Sunrise to...

An Autobiography by Mary Bertenshaw

A Vivid Personal
Account of her Life
in Manchester

Adapted
by
Alan Yardley

As Broadcast Originally by BBC
Radio Manchester in 1980

PRINTWISE PUBLICATIONS LTD
1991

© Published 1991 by PRINTWISE PUBLICATIONS LTD.
47 Bradshaw Road, Tottington, BURY, LANCS. BL8 3PW.

Warehouse and orders:—
40-42 Willan Industrial Estate, Vere Street,
(off Eccles New Road), SALFORD,
M5 2GR.
061-745 9168

© TEXT BY MARY BERTENSHAW/ALAN YARDLEY
Formerly Published under the same title in 1980.

Additional material and this reprint organised by

Cliff Hayes

ISBN No. 1 872226 18 3.

Printed and bound by Manchester Free Press, Paragon Mill, Jersey Street,
Manchester M4 6FP. Tel. 061-236 8822.

*If you have difficulty in obtaining copies
of this book or require copies by post
please send a cheque or p/o for £4.95
to include postage and packing to:*

CREATV

2 ENSTONE WAY
TYLDESLEY
MANCHESTER
M29 8WD

cheques made payable to Crea-TV

FOREWORD

I can vividly remember Mary Bertenshaw arriving at the BBC with a plastic carrier bag containing four loose-leaf folders. Mary had become a regular visitor to our studios in Manchester and had contributed to many of our programmes. She would drop in for a chat and a coffee and I would enjoy listening to the stories of her childhood in Manchester at the turn of the century.

"I thought you might be interested in this," she said, placing the carrier bag on my desk. Interested I was. The bag contained a copy of her newly completed autobiography "SUNRISE TO SUNSET". Four hundred and thirty type-written pages, describing her recollections of those childhood days.

I began the process of adapting the story for serialisation on BBC Radio Manchester, and found myself plunged into an era which to me, some forty-five years younger than the author, had been merely a page in a school history book.

The radio serialisation proved so popular that the story was published in book form. It quickly became a best seller and soon the book was out of print. Thousands of readers were disappointed, and despite the constant demand has, until now, remained unobtainable.

I would like to thank Cliff Hayes for organising this reprint, but most of all Mary Bertenshaw, for having the conviction to write it all down. I am sure you will get as much enjoyment from reading the book as I did.

Alan Yardley 1991

ACKNOWLEDGEMENTS

Grateful Thanks to:

Chris Makepeace, local historian, for help with the original book and also permission to reproduce pictures in this second edition.

Jim Stanhope-Brown for all his help and for kindly loaning the photos on pages 12, 28 & 54.

Front cover: picture of Angel Street, donated by kind permission of James Stanhope-Brown, author of 'Angels from the Meadow'. Inset: An early picture of Mary Bertenshaw.

ROCHDALE RD
Oldham Rd
Goods Sta.
Gasworks
Smithfield Mk
Fish Mk
SHUDE HILL
SWAN ST.
DANTZIC
BROMLEY ST.
PEARY ST.
BILBROOK ST.
GOULD ST.
LUDGATE HILL
LUDGATE ST.
THOMPSON ST.
BENDIX ST.
GOULDEN ST.
ADDINGTON ST.
CABLE ST.
MASON ST.
MARSHALL ST.
NEW CROSS
HARGREAVES ST.
CHASE ST.
CRABBE ST.
BRIGHTON ST.
Iron Wks
ANGEL ST.
ASPIN LA.
FACTORY LA.
SIMPSON ST.
DYCHE ST.
SHARP ST.
MAYES ST.
OSWALD ST.
OLDHAM RD
HENRY ST.
GEORGE LEIGH ST.

INTRODUCTION

The object of writing this book is to fulfil promises made over the years to my children and grandchildren to illustrate the many vivid memories of my early childhood (although some eighty years on dates may be a little out of focus occasionally). Living in a communal environment with thirty-two people is, to say the least, unusual to most children, and space prevents me from portraying all of them in the pages of this book. Here then in the sunset of my life is a small offering to my children grandchildren and great grandchildren. I hope it also gives joy to my 'darling' sisters Evelyn and Ellen, not forgetting 'baby' James Lionel.

In 1974 during one of my many calls to the phone-in on Radio Manchester, Sandra Chalmers, the presenter of the programme, urged me to put pen to paper. This spurred me on and I began to write down the first of what turned out to be over one hundred and thirty thousand words. Sandra, thanks.

When that original manuscript was completed some time later it was Alan Yardley, then a producer at Radio Manchester and now a television director, who adapted the book for radio serialisation and publication. Without Alan's help those torn and tattered pages would now be gathering dust. Thank you Alan for being a friend.

Mary Bertenshaw

THIS BOOKS IS DEDICATED TO:

My children:	Dorothy, Granville and Anthony.
Grandchildren:	Lorraine, Julie, Stephen, Christopher, Raymond and John.
and Great grandchildren:	Johnathan, Matthew, Paul, Debbie, Joanne, Christopher, Daniel and Jade.

# CONTENTS	Page

Foreword & Acknowledgements..................................3
Map of Angel Meadow..4
Introduction..5
To Manchester..7
My Wonderful Father..13
The Little Princess...17
A Young Quaker Girl..22
Nancy Dickiebird..29
Aunty Betsy Carter..36
To Angel Meadow...42
Traveller's Call...47
The Little Tin Box..53
Uncut Diamonds...58
Irish Paddy...64
The 'Half Inchers' and The 'Confidence Trickster'..........70
My First Boyfriend...76
Bandbox Lettie..80
Christmas 1913..85
Mary Anne...89
The Chicken Murderer..94
Another Sister...98
The Whit Walks...102
On The Move Again..106
My First Job...109
Another New Arrival...113
They say The Good Die Young................................117
The Unwanted Visitor..120
On My Own Again...124

CHAPTER 1

To Manchester

It was October the 3rd, 1909 when I came, at the age of five, to live for ever in Manchester.
My parents were Manchester people, who went to work in Buxton, Derbyshire, in the hotels there. The mineral Spa water was a great incentive to the wealthy class of people who were suffering from rheumatism.
As my parents were only young and had managed to get a small cottage, they were able to save a little money. Then, in 1904, I was born.
After living in Buxton for five years (where I was baptised at St. Anne's Church) they decided to come back home to Manchester. My mother was fretting for her relatives.
There was her father, her grandfather, her uncle John Henry, her aunt Theresa Ellen, young Theresa Ellen her cousin, besides her sister Lizzie, her sister Maggie and brothers Tommy and Jimmy.
My Dad wasn't as lucky as mother regarding relatives. He had no parents, his father dying at the age of 39. He had a brother William, who was a regular soldier in India; his aunt Betsey Carter and his cousins Lizzie McMullen and sister Jessie McMullen.
I was delighted at meeting all these relatives. They all made a tremendous fuss of me, and each in turn took me out somewhere - to the park to make daisy chains, to the fair on the dobby horses, or to Shudehill to see the cocks and hens and rabbits and pigeons on the stalls in their cotes.
After getting settled in, after about a month, Mother got a job at the laundry as "fancy ironer", which meant she put the "crinkles" in the frills of the white pinafores and hats that were worn by the housemaids and cooks who were in service.
Now all at once my life began. I loved Manchester right from the start.
Of course I was attending school, at St. Edmunds in Monsall Street, Miles Platting, the nearest Catholic school to where we lived in Collyhurst. Mother was working, and an elderly friend looked after me, and made sure that I reached school.
I wore my hair in a little "top knot" or bun on the top of my head

with one of Mother's hairpins pushed through to keep it in place. I wore a little pair of yellow clogs with red piping round the base which was held on by little brass studs. My hair was very dark and I wore golden sleeper earrings, which I had put in my ears when I was three years old. It was a family tradition that females should have their ears pierced to keep away evil or disease from the eyes! My Grandmothers on both my parents' sides believed in this superstition.

Mother's aunt Theresa Ellen visited us one day in Buxton and declared that now I was three it was time this operation took place. Of course, I hadn't a clue what was going on when my Mother lifted me upon her knee. Aunt Theresa Ellen came from behind quietly with needle, cotton and cork, and said very smoothly "now keep very quiet then you can go and see the German band after I've finished".

I didn't see what she had in her hand; she made sure of that because I would have screamed the house down. It was painful and both ears were complete with cotton earrings in no time. With the aid of a bit of spit, proper earrings could be put in within a week. As promised, both Mother and Aunt Theresa Ellen took me up the street to see the German band; the men with their pierrot hats and pantaloons.

Buxton was behind us now. It was very quiet in comparison to Collyhurst. I began to collect new little friends.

I was beginning to feel very important too, and I could feel myself growing up. One of the reasons for this was because Mrs Lomas, the lady who looked after me, got to sending me on the odd errand to the

The little house in Buxton where I was born in 1904.

Rochdale Road, at the corner of Angel St.

corner shop. I often went for two penn'orth of blackcurrant jam in a little Wedgwood jug, and another thing I used to like doing was to take a jug to the milkman who would fill it with a ladle out of a huge zinc container, or it may have been buttermilk which was lovely and sour and curdly, and great for Mother's skin or for making scones.

I would go with my friends into the park on Cheltenham Street, on the swings, or playing ropes or shuttlecock and paddle. Shuttlecock was my favourite. You could get a lovely green feathered shuttlecock for a penny, or a red or blue one. If you had more than one, you could mix the feathers and it looked lovely when you threw it in the air. Whip and top was my next favourite because it had the same effect colour-wise. We would keep any nice coloured paper especially for our tops. A piece of red off the Handy Brand condensed milk can, or a piece of the green, gold and black off a penny packet of Woodbines. We didn't have any particular pattern; we would just stick on a bit of each colour on the little wooden top, then twist it onto the ground and Hey Presto! circles of beautiful rainbow rings.

These were very happy days. Tram rides with Dad on a Sunday, and aunties and uncles all over the place!

1911

The year 1911 was an eventful year for me. It was the year of the Coronation of George and Mary, and it was also the year of my first Holy Communion, as I had reached my seventh birthday. Another very happy event was also going to happen. At least so Mother said. She told me that she had ordered a baby. Both of these happenings turned out to be terrible disappointments to me. First was the Coronation Party.

On the morning of the Coronation, Mother came into my bedroom. to wake me up for school. As I turned to answer her, she cried,

"Good Heavens, what's wrong with you, you're covered in spots!" Yes, I'd got measles.

"Well," said Mother, "you can't go to school". How awful, I'd miss the Coronation Party!

"But I want to go to school, they're having a party and giving us a box of chocolates". Needless to say, I didn't go to school but was kept nice and warm in bed. There was one nice thing though. Mother had promised to go to the school to see about the goodies I didn't want to miss, and they sent them to our house. Later, I was lying in bed with the window open when I heard a voice say

"Are you going to see the illuminated tram?"

"Oh, yes of course!" the other voice answered.

I remembered this was going to be the biggest treat of all and yet I wouldn't be able to see it. It was to pass Collyhurst Street at a certain time, I've forgotten what time, but I do remember shouting "Mam" in order to ask her was she going, but there was no answer. Then it dawned on me that they must have slipped to the road to see the tram and I thought that I would do the same; so I got dressed and set off on my journey. Everyone seemed to be staring at me, but as I had not seen a mirror, I'd no idea what I looked like.

I trotted along and stood in the doorway of Slater's shop at the bottom of Collyhurst Street. I was only a few yards from my Mother and her friend Mrs Lomas although I didn't know it. Two of my friends came and stood by the shop doorway with their mother, but they didn't know I was there until I said

"Hello Annie". They turned round.

"What's wrong with your face?" says Annie. "You should be in bed, you've got measles", said Mrs Keyes.

"I know", I said innocently.

"You know?", bellowed Mrs Keys. "Well, what are you doing here if you know?"

"I've come to see the tram", I said.

Mrs Keys hurried off with the girls as though vultures were after her. I had only been there about ten minutes when my Mother arrived. Mrs Keys met her and told her where I was.

"Come on back home, quick!" said Mother, and off I was taken. I started to cry, but Mother was sympathetic, saying

"Yes, I know. it is a shame, but if you get a chill, you might die".

This frightened me, but I did promise on the Infant Jesus that I would stay in bed until she went to see the tram. I kept my promise, and I didn't get a chill; far from it, as it was summer-time and I was wearing a red flannel nightie which was rather overpowering.

It was some months after the Coronation when Mother was getting the clothes ready for the new baby. I noticed all the preparations were well under way.

"Have you got enough money for the new baby now?", I asked.

"Yes, I think so," said Mother.

"What time are they sending it?" I asked.

"We'll have to wait and see," said Mother.

When I got home the next day I heard the sad news. Mother had had the baby, a girl, but it was dead. "Big Lizzie" the woman who cleaned at the local pub was the woman in attendance at the birth.

I was very upset at hearing that had the baby lived, I would have had my very own little sister. Mother was kept in bed and had to be quiet, which was very hard for the children outside - we who spent every waking moment in the streets with skipping ropes, whips and tops, bobbers and kibs, shuttlecocks - oh! there was no end to the playing. But I was too sad to play.

Anyway, I was very pleased about one thing. I was taken by Mrs Lomas into the back kitchen to have a look at the baby before it got buried. It was rolled up in a white blanket, showing just its face, and was lying on the back-board of our very large iron mangle in the corner by the slop-stone. I couldn't see the baby for the very large wheel at the side of the mangle, so Mrs Lomas had to lift me up. It was put there to be kept cool away from the fire. I began to cry and said

"Why did it die?" I suppose being a mother herself, she had to be equipped with the art of very quick thinking where an inquisitive child was concerned. She answered

"Oh it's very sad, but the baby caught cold".

Little Scotland. This road is now called Corporation St., but in 1910 it was a continuation of Long Millgate. These houses were just to the side of what is now Parker's Hotel.

"What, on its way from Heaven?" I asked.
"That's right, it's a long journey", she said.
"Well, why didn't God look after it?" I asked. There was a pause - as well equipped as she was, she must have been stumped on this one - at least I don't remember the answer.
I was again, at seven, the only child.

CHAPTER 2

My Wonderful Father

Although I absolutely worshipped my Father, at the same time, I lived in awe of him. It was not fear. It was a sort of feeling that he knew everything. I felt that he even knew when I'd been naughty.

I had been lost at the Wakes one day. I'd travelled there on my own. It was on Albert Memorial Croft, around the corner. My mother and Mrs Lomas (who minded me when my Mum was at work), had already taken me on the Saturday previously and I was told not to go on my own, but I didn't take much notice of my Mother and I trotted off.

It was the Summer Wakes, so that meant light evenings. I was enthralled looking at the big lads showing off their skill and muscles by throwing wooden balls at the coconuts and knocking them down and people throwing their hoopla rings in the hope of winning a prize from the table. There was so much fairground music, all different tunes all going together - from the peacock round-about; the great huge swing boat and the big horses, and dozens of other things - so that you couldn't hear your own ears. But, it was lovely musical music, not like the juke box music of today. Although I was absolutely mesmerised and delighted at the big wooden horses with their wild eyes, open mouths, and great leaping ability, I was too young and small to be allowed on them. Anyway, it was a penny a ride on them, and I only had a penny in my pinny pocket. I didn't know whether to buy a toffee apple, or a halfpenny cornet. Finally, I decided to go on the little dobbie horses, and, after spending up and seeing every single thing on the fair, I decided to go home and made my way out. There were hundreds of people about, many of them lost children, and I had to squeeze and squeeze past them to get out. But I didn't seem to be making any headway and I kept telling myself "I passed that before". I went round in circles. I was never a crying child, and was normally capable of acting like an older child. Today was different. I was locked in amongst hundreds of people it seemed. I could only keep pushing against men's legs and getting caught in the long skirts of the women. I was wearing my hair in two short plaits, and somewhere on the fairground floor were two red ribbons. My fringe was stuck to my forehead. I was gasping for breath, it was boiling hot weather.

14   *SUNRISE TO SUNSET*

My wonderful father

I wondered about the other children I'd seen. Were they in the same predicament? I suddenly remembered that I should have done as I was told by my mother. I never gave my Father a thought. When I realised that I could breath again, I found myself on Queen's Road. I was only a few yards from the Street on which I travelled to school, but I was bewildered, so I asked a lady - "Please could you tell me the way to Cheltenham Street?" The lady said,"Well, look luv, you will either have to go through the Wakes or go all the way down Rochdale Road, and you'll probably get lost". I felt panic-stricken. "I can't go through the Wakes that's how I got lost", I said. The lady took my hand and said kindly, "I'll tell you what, we'll find a policeman".

We walked to the corner of Queen's Road and Rochdale Road where we found two policemen.

"Officer, I've just found this little girl lost", said the lady.

"This is little Mary from Cheltenham Street isn't it," replied a very fair-skinned policeman known as "Baby Face".

"They've been looking all over for you," said the other policeman.

"She's been missing three hours", said Baby Face looking at the lady.

"We'll take her home, come on Mary - thank you Mrs".

As it was a sunny summer, everyone from every house seemed to be talking at their doors. When I came into view, there seemed to be smiles in their hundreds, besides nods and winks for the policeman.

Our house was straight opposite Willert Street Police Station, and although I only knew "Baby Face", all the policemen knew me, because of my dancing around the barrel organ.

When we got to our door, Mother and Mrs Lomas were very pale and nearly crying when they saw me. Mother put out her arms, "thank you very much officer," but the policeman wouldn't let me go.

"I can't let you have her yet, you see I'll have to verify that she has been found". By six o' clock, I was allowed to go home.

I was hungry, thirsty, tired, dirty and a little bad tempered. The kettle was boiling on the hob with evidently not much water in it, as you could hear the marble running around inside. The fire was very low and the table was laid for tea.

"Take off your clogs, and where's your ribbons?" says Mother.

"Bring some water Eva, and I'll wash her hands and face," she said to Mrs Lomas's daughter.

"I don't want my face washing - I'm hungry," for once I cried.

"You can't eat anything in that state," says Mother.

She put in front of me a plate with two slices of pressed home-cooked sheep's head and a nice red tomato which I ate in no time, washing it down with a cup of milk.

After I had finished the meal, I was put to bed, for once not minding a bit. I wanted to go to sleep, but I could hear an odd raised word from downstairs. Words like "Jim" (who was my father), and "smacked bottom". This argument I realised was about me, so I got out of bed and sat on the stairs in my nightie listening.

Mother's voice was saying:-

"Good heavens, she's only seven".

"I know, she's made her first Communion, which means she's old enough to use reason, and should know right from wrong".

"Well, I don't want Jim to know," said my Mother.

"That's where you make the mistake with her; Jim should know, he'd smack her backside."

"I doubt it," said Mother.

"What about when she was missing in Buxton - cleared off to the woods instead of going into school. She terrified me to death. Hairy Mary's crawling up the curtains - dozens of caterpillars she brought home in a paper bag," says Mrs Lomas.

"What about the time when Jim bought her those yellow clogs and tammy-shanter. She played 'wag' then, didn't she?" There she was admiring her earrings and clogs in the mirror in the jeweller's doorway, instead of school. I think it's time that Jim took over," she says.

During this conversation, I began to realise how lucky I was that my Father wasn't at home, he was at work. He worked as door-keeper at the Osborne Theatre on Oldham Road, for his leg trouble didn't allow him to do any heavy manual work.

The argument seemed to have stopped so I went back to bed and was soon fast asleep.

The days passed by in the usual way. There was the daily attendance at school; Church on Sundays and the pictures at Dickie Bank's little cinema in Gay Street on a Sunday afternoon.

Although I was brought up a Catholic, all my little regular friends, apart from Madelaine, were Protestants, so I used to go with them to the Gay Street Mission where we used to see the most beautiful Holy Bible pictures projected from the magic lantern. We would then go home, and if our tea wasn't ready, we'd ask for a sugar buttie or maybe a condensed milk one or a jam one. There was always more than one child eating butties in the street.

Nearly every day, somewhere in one street or another we would see or hear the barrel organ. It was heaven on earth for children in those days. Our organ man came from Jersey Street, Ancoats, and we loved him, not only the children, but our Mums and Grans also. As the houses were just two up and two down, you felt you were still in your own kitchen, if you sat on your own front step when the organ man came along.

Mrs Morley, a very stout lady who seemed to be always sitting on the step, would say to him "Put it on number four and Mary will dance." Number four was "She's got rings on her fingers and bells on her toes", and I would dance like an Hawaaian, while everyone clapped.

Mother used to give the man a drink of tea; I used to like that because it meant that I could bring out our little stool; stand on it, and turn the handle of the organ to keep the music playing, but it didn't sound half as nice when I did it. There was the secret of turning the handle, otherwise you got a clug-clug sound in the tune instead of an even rhythm. No-one bothered, not even the organ man who was too busy drinking his tea. Everyone smiled and we all had great fun!

CHAPTER 3

The Little Princess

After getting lost at the Wakes, I tried to make sure I didn't tread on Mrs Lomas's toes again. I was "coming to the age of reason", a Catholic phrase relating to a child of seven, and I was beginning to realise that I hadn't been very fair to Mrs Lomas. I was trying to be good and do whatever I was told, but I wasn't having much success. Until that is Lizzie took me home to see her doll.

Mrs Lomas had been struggling to light the fire under the old brick-boiler so she could do the washing. The bucket of coal which she had brought in from the yard the night before was still damp. She had tried three times and each time it had gone out. Not only that, but the wood had burned away. I was having breakfast when I heard her say:

"I detest Monday mornings."

"Why?" I asked.

"This rotten washing," she said.

"Why don't you work in the laundry with my Mum?" I asked.

"I'm not as clever as your Mam," she said, "besides, who'd mind you?"

I hadn't thought about this. Who would mind me? Mother wouldn't be able to work, and she liked her job as "fancy ironer". Not only that, but she needed the money as my Father didn't seem to keep a job long owing to his disability.

Mrs Lomas got the scraper and began frantically - and I think rather bad-temperedly - to scrape out the coal and sticks again. Before my Mother had left for work, her last remark was "Don't put your pinny on until the last minute." Our pinnies were always shining white, and mine were always especially lovely because Mother ironed them at the laundry, and she didn't want me to dirty it before I reached school.

I was just opening the button on the basque and undoing the tape on the neck at the back of the pinny when Mrs Lomas said "I'll be here all day, this coal's no good. Go and see if Ivy, who was my friend, will go with you for a quarter of coal".

"I don't want to go for coal," I said.

"There's nothing you do want to do unless it's just to suit you," she said.

"I've got my clean pinny on, you go for the coal," I said as I dashed out.

Dad was in bed when I went out and didn't know about the episode. But, by gum, he knew all about it, and so did I, by the time I got home that afternoon.

On my way from school, I had met my "going to school" friend, little Lizzie Harrison. She said that she had a doll for her birthday which actually closed its eyes. She promised to show it to me if I would go with her to her house, which meant us crossing the length of the whole croft until we reached the Churnet Street end of Rochdale Road. Finally we reached her house. There was a lovely smell of cooking.

I watched Lizzie as she bent down to pick up her doll which she handled with the greatest of care. She handed her to me. I knew that I had never seen anything so beautiful in my life. It did close its eyes. It had on a lovely hat and shoes, and even white drawers underneath, just like the ones Lizzie and I and every other little girl wore. I was transfixed, and Lizzie, thinking that she might not get the doll back, said "Can I have her back now?"

I handed back the doll gently, as though it was really a lovely baby. Suddenly the door burst open and in dashed Lizzie's brother Tom.

"Here's our Tom." said Lizzie's Mother Mrs Harrison. I had a feeling that she was hinting that now Tom was home, they were ready for tea, and I should go home, so I turned towards the door to go.

"I'm going now Lizzie, see you on the croft tomorrow," I said.

"All right," said Lizzie.

I put my hand on the door to open it when Lizzie's Mother said, "Like a piece of apple pie before you go?" Well, what a thing to ask any child in those days!

"Yes please," I said meekly, trying to make it look as though it wasn't unusual for me to be eating apple pie. It was delicious, with lovely sugar sprinkled on top. Lizzie couldn't have any, because her Mother said it would spoil her tea, so whilst I was tucking in, Lizzie had picked up her doll again;

"Aren't her eyes a lovely colour?" she said.

"Her hair is the same colour as yours," I said. Lizzie was fair with a beauty spot on her cheek.

"I wish I was like her though." said Lizzie.

"So do I, she's like a little princess," I wistfully remarked.

"Come on little princess, - you'd better get off home, your Mother will be wondering where you are. Go with her Lizzie, as far as the corner." said Mrs Harrison.

Lizzie left me near "The Three Tuns" in Churnet Street, after saying "Ta, Ta, see you on the croft tomorrow".

I couldn't forget that lovely doll. My birthday had been two months before, so I would have to wait until Christmas. Lizzie's doll cost four shillings. Father Christmas might not want to spend all that much just on me; what about all his other children, and hospitals too. Anyway, if I'm good, I might get one, I thought. If I'm good! I am glad Mother told Mrs Lomas not to tell my Dad on me last week. Oh gosh! I'd forgotten about the coal episode this morning. I began to hope that Mrs Lomas would have forgotten too.

As I was passing the corner shop opposite Robertshaw's Works, I noticed their clock said six o'clock. I had to bend down to take my clogs off to shake the cinders out of them which always got in on Albert Croft. No-one seemed to be about. I was leaning on one elbow on the wooden window cill of the shop whilst I worked the button on my right clog into the hole of the strap. I noticed how the little flame kept popping out of the hole in the mantle which was on the gas bracket on the inside of the window. I'd just put my foot down when the lady came out of the shop kitchen which was opposite the window. She saw me and said "You'll get murdered when you get home. You haven't gone over that croft have you?"

"No. I've been to Lizzie's." I said.

"Who's Lizzie?" she asked.

"My friend," I replied.

"Well, the police and your Dad are on the croft looking for you." she spoke accusingly.

I dashed home, hoping to run into my Mother's arms. I ran and I ran. Although it was only two minutes away, it seemed miles and miles.

Finally, I reached our door, number 87 and banged, shouting, "Mam, Mam, open the door." The door opened immediately. My Mother looked very pale and so did Mrs Lomas. I didn't know that you went pale through worry. Well, I'd never experienced worry. I didn't know what the word meant. I just thought they needed some senna tea (which was always stewing in a jug in the oven) or maybe castor oil. Mother gave me senna mostly when I went pale. I know she would take one look at me and say "You're pale. Have you been on the lavatory today? Right, take this." giving me half a cup of senna tea.

Mother met me as I knew she would with open arms.

"Are you home early?" I asked.

"Yes, the police came for me, we thought you were lost."

"You little bugger," hissed Mrs Lomas, as I looked over at her.

"All right, she'll get enough of that off Jim." said Mother. But why should I be afraid of my Dad? He had never laid a hand on me. Dad wouldn't touch me.

"Where have you been. Why didn't you come home from school?" my Mother asked.

"I went to see Lizzie Harrison's doll. Oh Mam, you should see it, it's lovely. Can I have one for Christmas?"

"Who's Lizzie Harrison?" asked Mother.

"My friend," I said.

"I didn't know you had a friend named Lizzie. I know Ivy, and Lily and Madelaine, but not Lizzie," she said.

"Well, she's not my 'special friend'" I said, "just a girl I know who comes over the croft to go to school."

"Well, anyway, you're home. Don't ever go anywhere again before you come home," said Mother.

"I won't," I said.

"By gum! you'll have something to tell the Priest next time you go to Confession," said Mrs Lomas.

"Don't go and side with Jim when he comes in,"'says Mother to Mrs Lomas.

"I don't think anyone will have any need to side with Jim," said Mrs Lomas, giving me a black look. "Maybe something will be done about her behaving herself this time."

I wasn't afraid of Dad coming in, not now Mother was there anyway. Everything would be all right. Then there was a "Knock,knock" on the door. Up jumps Mrs Lomas and in walks Dad and the policeman. The policeman was all smiles, but I couldn't tell how Dad looked.

"Where've you bin, eh?" he asked.

"To Lizzie's," I said.

"Who's Lizzie?" And the whole story had to be recounted again. I was getting tired of having to repeat it. What is wrong with going to your friend's house, anyway? Finally, the policeman went. I was glad he'd gone, because I thought that was the end of it. Until Dad spoke!

"Come here." he said. I walked very slowly towards him.

"Why didn't you come straight home from school?" he asked.

I didn't want to repeat the story again but I thought that if I altered it, I may be found out in a lie, and Dad hated liars. So I began......."I went to Lizzie's......

"Lizzie who, Lizzie who?" said Dad impatiently. At that point Mother intervened.

"Oh a friend of hers - don't frighten her." she said.

"Don't frighten her! It's through you she's ruined," snaps Dad.

"What do you mean?" said Mother in a surprised voice.

"Well for one thing, according to the policeman she was lost on the fair in August. You didn't tell me about that did you? And what about the coal this morning. You wouldn't go for Mrs Lomas, would you?" he said straight at me.

"Well, you had to tell him." said Mother to Mrs Lomas.

"Well, yes I did Polly." (addressing Mother by her pet name), "but I never expected all this trouble again today. I just thought he should talk to her."

Dad spoke, "Now this is going to be the last of this. I've lost a night's work, maybe even my job through being off tonight, so I'll have to teach you a lesson." Almost immediately he said this, he tipped me over his knee and threw up my frock (a red cashmere frock with white honeycomb stitching across the front). Underneath I wore a white flannel petticoat and a pair of red flannel drawers which were made up of two separate legs on a waistband, so that when he bent me over, the cheeks of my bottom were exposed to the elements and I began to scream and kick, but Dad won. He smacked my bottom until it burned. His own hands must have hurt. When he had finished I stood up and he took hold of the end of my pinafore to keep me in one place until he had finished talking. I tried to keep my back to him, mostly from shame and humiliation, than disobedience.

"Look at me when I talk to you," he said. I looked at him, but my eyes filled up. I couldn't believe he didn't love me any less than my Mother did.

"You didn't like that, did you?" he asked. I nodded, with a "No".

"Well," he said, "that's nothing to what you'll get if I ever hear of you giving Mrs Lomas, or anyone else cheek. Always remember, she was a little girl once and had to do as she was told."

This was a lesson from my father I never forgot.

CHAPTER 4

A Young Quaker Girl

I began to see the light almost as soon as my Father gave me the thrashing. My little friend Madelaine, who, incidentally, was a very beautiful child according to all the neighbours, lived in a little house on the edge of the croft. As she was in my class, I would call for her on my way to school. The day after my beating I called as usual.

I knocked on the door and her Mother opened it. "Is Madelaine coming to school?" I asked.

"Madelaine is going to school - what happened to you yesterday? I'll bet you won't play wag again will you?" she said. I nodded my head, meaning "No".

"Don't be teaching our Madelaine how to play wag." she said. Whilst she was saying this, Madelaine squeezed past her Mother at the same time putting on the other half of her coat. She said "Ta-ta" to her Mother and we set off for school.

Off we went walking towards Queen's Road, to go to Saint Edmund's School in Monsall Street. After a while, Madelaine said "Why didn't you go straight home from school yesterday?"

"I went to Lizzie Harrison's to see her doll," I said.

"I heard you were missing until half past six" she said.

"It was six o'clock," I said very sheepishly.

"It wasn't, it was half past six, me Mam said so," said Madelaine.

"Well, it was six o'clock by Brown's clock in the shop window."

"Oh, it's always six o'clock by that; everyone thought a bogey-man had pinched you," she said.

So that was it! Everyone must have been talking about me, and after what Dad did I wasn't likely to do anything like that again.

I never did find out who went for the quarter of coal. And surprisingly, Mrs Lomas was very nice to me before I left for school. But she didn't forget to warn me though, all the same, did she? I always came straight home from school after that episode. I suppose it seems funny to some people when children do these things but for their own sakes, someone has to be firm. I never played wag again.

Dad was up when I arrived home from school. This was unusual. He didn't usually get up until five o'clock at night.

"I suppose he's got up in case he's needed for a search party." I thought to myself, thinking of yesterday's thrashing. He was just putting the cat down on to the floor from off his chair and had his back to me. I was a bit nervous of what he would say when he turned around. He knew I'd come in. I sat on the steel stool, which stood with its two back legs in the fender, without saying a word. Slowly, he turned round.

"Well, did you like school today," he asked. I didn't answer, but raised my eye-brows, puckered out my lips and nodded a "yes".

"That's a good girl," he said. That was my Dad. There was no fuss from my Dad - just honesty.

Whilst Dad worked at the Osborne Theatre, he was able to get complimentary tickets, which meant we could go straight in, instead of queueing. I used to love to see Wee Georgie Wood, the little man who was always a boy. I also used to love to see the chorus girls dancing. There was always a lot of tap dancing then, and the comedians were often made up with their hair plastered down and their faces and noses painted. They nearly always had baggy trousers, mostly in a loud check or a diamond pattern, and wore funny long braces.

We used to love to go to the Pantomime, especially to see Dick Whittington and his Cat. I got very upset at the Babes in the Wood show, when the wicked uncle left them to die. By the time they played "God save the King", I was heartbroken, until all the cast came on together, and I saw that the children were safe, then I was very happy. I used to like to read all the advertisements on the big heavy fire curtain. Advertisements such as "Doans Backache and Kidney Pills", "Pear's Transparent Soap", and "Swan Vesta Matches". I used to read them whilst we waited for Dad finishing his jobs, such as locking the exit doors, tipping up the seats, then putting out the little gas lights on the walls of the theatre. The treat went on for ages. I didn't always go with my Mother. Sometimes she would want to iron or bake, in which case, she would give her ticket to Mrs Lomas. Dad even managed to get tickets for Aunt Theresa Ellen, or Uncle John Henry, or my Grandad.

Sometime around then, there was a lot of excitement because a new picture house called the Empress opened on the next block to the Osborne Theatre. You could actually hear the noise of the train on the film! The age of enlightenment! So that was life then. A night at the Osborne; a night at the Empress and then a night at the Queen's Park Hippodrome, and of them all, my favourite was the Queen's Park Hip!

I went to Saint Edmund's School all the time I lived in Collyhurst and around this time we had a little musical performance of "The Quaker Girl" on the stage of the Queen's Park Hip. It would be 1912. I was

Charter St., (then Blakely St.), note the houses and the Ragged School on the far right.

a Quaker girl, and there were girls in green capes too, but I don't know what they were supposed to be.

All our parents were there, Mother and Mrs Lomas sitting right on the front row, near the orchestra. As it was a special occasion, they'd spent hours getting ready. I remember Mother hurriedly trying to curl her hair with the curling tongs. She pushed them through the bars of the fire for a while, then with a rag in her hand pulled them out, spat on her finger and touched the tongs quickly. It sizzled, and made little bubbles which rolled about on the tongs. Then, she got a small amount of hair in one hand and wrapped it around the tongs. There was an awful smell of burning hair.

"Polly," said Mrs Lomas, "You're burning your hair!"

"Yes, I know," said Mother, scraping off the hair that had stuck to the tongs. A couple of more tries and she was complete with bun at the back and curly fringe at the front. She gently dipped a little bit of cotton wool into the small box which contained carmine powder, and very smoothly touched both cheeks. I thought she looked lovely. My mother was noted for her good looks. Her hair was jet black and she had the most beautiful eyes of deepest blue. We were all set. especially Mrs Lomas in her bottle green costume with leg o'mutton sleeves and frilly jabot. We finally arrived at the theatre where the children were taken in hand by the teacher and taken behind the scenes.

When the orchestra had found their places, the fiddles or violins and other instruments would begin to tune up, and everyone would become tense with excitement. Then the orchestra would play the introduction to the story.

The girls in the capes came on first with some boys. Then the quaker girls came on dancing with their boys. I remember that it had been on for quite a long time when the boyfriends of the green cape girls had to kneel on one knee and sit their girlfriends on the other knee. Everything was going fine when one little girl called Maggie Norton who lived in the 'Three Tuns' slipped off the knee of Frankie Lee, and fell on to the floor. Our teacher looked petrified, but all the audience and the children in the wings were roaring with laughter. Frank started again but bent the wrong knee and had to start again, causing uproars of laughter. Even the teacher lost her embarrassment and had to laugh. Eventually, everything started to go smoothly. My next appearance was when the green capes and the Quaker girls and all the boys were assembled on the stage. The Quaker girls wore green linen dresses with white spotted organdie aprons, a little pea-green bonnet with white organdie front and black shoes and stockings, and as we held hands with the boys, they looked at us and sang:

> "I like your apron and your bonnet
> And your little Quaker dress
> You're modest and demure
> And you really look your best;
> And when you're out on Sunday
> Everytime I look at you,
> I always feel I'd like to be
> A little Quaker too."

We both bowed gently to one another, but maybe I didn't bow gently enough, because as I bent, I felt a crack somewhere along my waist.

Before I realised what had happened, first one red flannelette leg, then the other, began to show beneath my dress. My drawers were falling down. As I was not far from the wings at the side, I was hoping teacher would come and help me.

I looked pitifully down towards my Mother and Mrs Lomas, but by the look on their faces, you would have thought maybe their drawers had fallen down too! I heard a "Sssss", which was teacher trying to catch my attention. I looked around and she beckoned for me to come to her side.

By now, the frills that should have been around my knees were around my ankles. Finally, I bent down and grabbed my clothes anywhere, just to keep my legs in, and I rushed off the stage. The fall of a great star! When I finally reached the side, I realised that the whole place was howling with laughter. I could not laugh. I wondered why it had to be me that had to be wearing a pair of drawers that wouldn't keep on. I was afraid to look at my Mother. I thought she'll be thinking "Trust Mary to do the wrong thing".

When teacher had found a safety pin and fastened me up again, I thought I would chance a peep at my Mother, but Mother and Mrs Lomas were turned to a lady behind them who seemed to be doing all the talking. As her face was towards the stage, she noticed me and nudged Mother to look. To my amazement both she and Mrs Lomas smiled and gave a tiny wave of just the fingers. Phew! What a relief.

I was a bit dubious of how my Dad would take it, when he heard. Anyhow, by the time Mother came to tell him, everyone thought it had been great fun. "Well," said Dad, "she'll never make an actress. I think the only stage Mary will get on will be the landing stage carrying parcels!" He ruffled my hair affectionately with his hands and said smilingly "Poor little Mary".

The Christmas Wakes Fair came again for the holidays. For a couple of days before it actually opened, we would notice a few things, like the boat swings, with the thick coloured cotton rope which you would pull hard in order to be taken up and down in the air, and maybe a few stalls all covered in tarpaulin. As time went on, more and more things would arrive until the whole of the croft was covered. Then, the moments of magic. Music, brilliant lights! There would be shouting from the boxing booth by the man who promised you the earth if you could knock out the "boxer", who would be standing on the platform with a big square face and an ugly flat nose. Dad, Grandfather and Uncle John Henry enjoyed the boxing, whilst Mother, Mrs Lomas and I watched the man and the lady dolls on the organ box. The man usually had a drum and sticks, the lady a bell and hammer, and they would play their instruments to the fairground music. At least, that's what you thought. My other favourites were the hoopla stalls, where you had to throw a wooden ring over a prize to win.

In between fairs coming and going, we would have our own hoopla stalls. We would collect any thing from a shoe buckle to a crayon or fancy button, to a humbug on a bit of paper. Any small thing at all in fact. We would draw chalk squares to place them in, and we would have lots of wire rings. Goodness knows where we managed to get the wire from. But, like the lady on the fair, we would stand with a stick pushed inside the rings ready to take them off one at a time. Then we would shout, "Hoopla again here, two rings one pin, anything you win you have." We didn't have a counter, but had to kneel on the floor. Our frocks were always covered with pins in this game.

It was about this time that I began to realise that there was some truth in the fact that times really were much happier if you obeyed your Mother and Father.

It was whilst we were playing hoopla that we heard of a terrible tragedy. the sinking of the Titanic. But we weren't really interested and only picked up what adults said about it. Had it been today, all the scenes at sea would have been shown on television, but then, well, we had to form our own pictures from the excitement of the paper lad shouting "Extra, Extra. Read all about it - Titanic's been sunk, Titanic's been sunk." These "Extras" were always printed quickly if anything happened suddenly and were sold like hot cakes. The things which formed the picture in our young minds would be exclamations such as "Good God!", followed by "Fancy all those poor souls being drowned." Apart from that, the adults didn't enlarge much upon worldly things. It seemed children should be seen and not heard. It came to me one day that some people were more concerned than others when a while after the event, my Father came in with a black square made of silk, with white blocks printed upon it, with a black spot in the middle of the block. It was exactly like a headscarf of today, but this was a mourning symbol for the ship and was called a "Titanic".

My Dad was very smart with nice shirts when he was dressed, but on this occasion when he went out in his suit and bowler hat with silver watch and chain, he took out his white linen handkerchief from his chest pocket and replaced it with the Titanic square. Soon, however, this period of mourning was over, and the square was used to put over Gaby, his favourite canary, to stop her from singing at bedtime.

Christmas had been and gone. Easter was on its way, and with it the "walks". I "walked" in a white muslin dress made by Auntie Maggie. We children used to have our own May Queen procession and I was once the Queen. My Mother let me take off my clogs and put on my Sunday shoes which were boots fastened at the side with buttons. I put on my white dress, which I had worn for the church procession in May, but with the addition of a pink sash around my waist. Mother pinned on my head a long Nottingham lace curtain and placed a little wire wreath of paper flowers on my head, all held together with Mother's hairpins. My two little friends, Ivy and Lily both held each end of the lace veil to keep it from trailing on the floor. Next, two other little girls were given a garf. This was a wooden ring which had been taken from an orange or an apple barrel. The garf was also decorated with paper flowers and held at each side by two children, with the Queen underneath. All the other little girls wore paper aprons and banana bonnets. We would sing a song, and the children with a ribboned pole would dance around being careful not to pull hard enough to tear the ribbons off.

We would go very, very carefully from house to house with the Queen giving a gentle knock on each door. As soon as the door opened, we would begin to sing (to the tune of God Bless the Prince of Wales):-

> "Around this merry maypole
> Through the live long day,
> For gentle Mary Brown
> Is crowned the Queen of May.
> With hearts and voices ringing,
> We'll merrily praise the day,
> For gentle Mary Brown
> Is crowned the Queen of May."

We may not always have sung the words properly, but we didn't mind. Of course we collected as we went along, and afterwards, we would go to Mycock's shop for cakes, pop, tiger nuts and other nice things and have a party in someone's brown-stoned backyard on the large doorstep by the coal hole.

But like Cinderella, as soon as the party was over, off came my Sunday shoes and frock, and once again I was plain and simple "Cloggie".

CHAPTER 5

Nancy Dickiebird

My childhood was a time of fairytale days of fairgrounds, barrel organs, the moving picture man Dickie Banks, and May Queens. But there was also another very colourful person causing great excitement in the neighbourhood. Dear old Nancy.

Our little houses had no halls or lobbies. Our street was one of the longest in Collyhurst. I'd say that there were at least fifteen houses on each block. As you went to, or came home from school, you'd see through every single window a square wood-top table in the centre of the floor. Some would have on a nice fringed table-cloth, but on most there would be an oilcloth in one of the many pretty designs available. However, in several instances, there would be the last edition of the previous day's "Evening News" or "Chronicle" doing just as good a job. We were lucky. We had a table with a fringed tablecloth, and I was sitting at that table when I first saw Nancy.

It was a Saturday afternoon when I was having tea. I was sitting with my back to the window with Dad. Mother and Mrs Lomas were sitting opposite us looking towards the window, when Mother said "There's poor Nancy again. I wonder why they can't leave her alone."

"She's very quiet today, isn't she?" said Mrs Lomas. When I looked around, I saw a woman in the arms of two men. One a policeman and the other in plain clothes.

"That's Metcalfe," said Mother, meaning the detective.

"Come on, there's nothing for you to see,"said Dad to me. I was going to ask what she had done but thought better of it as Dad was a great believer in the saying "Children should be seen and not heard".

The incident soon passed from my mind and I forgot all about Nancy. Every day was so full of adventure. The nice weather had arrived and we were big enough to go on our own to Queen's Park up Rochdale Road.

We found the interesting game of making daisy or dandelion chains by putting a tiny split in the stalk of the first flower with our nail then gently putting the stalk of the next flower in the split. We'd repeat this with every flower, and the chains would grow and grow. We used to come home decked like South Sea island maidens with daisies around our heads and wrists, and dandelions around our necks. We used to spend hours doing that.

One day, a few of us had just got into our street from the park. We had been listening and dancing to the brass band and bathing in the water in front of the museum. We were making towards our house when all at once we heard a woman screaming "Leave me alone, leave me alone." Suddenly, from around the corner, came Nancy being held up by two policemen again.

I flew into our house and banged the door behind me.

"I'm frightened of her," I said.

"You've no need to be frightened of Nancy; she won't harm you," said my Mother, "she'll be singing her head off soon, when she cools down."

Just out of curiosity, I went with Lily and Ivy up to Willert Street Police Station to hear if she was singing, and before we got anywhere near the door, we could hear this beautiful voice. We carried on right to the Station door where two or three policemen were discussing something in the yard.

"What do you want?" one of the policemen said. "Have you come to hear Nancy sing?"

We just said "Yes" then, after a while, we went back home. When I got in, I said to my Mother, "Nancy was singing. She can sing nice."

"Yes, that's why they call her Nancy Dickiebird," said Mother. And she sang like that every weekend.

One Saturday, late in the afternoon, we were playing skipping in the middle of the road - you could do that in those days. No cars or buses in the ordinary street. Only couldn't-care-less horses. Ivy had one end of the rope and Lily the other; I was jumping in the middle and we were saying:-

> "Doctor Foster's a very nice man,
> He teaches the children all he can,
> Reading, Writing and Arithmetic,
> But he doesn't forget to use his stick."

We'd just got to the last word when we heard a commotion. It was poor Nancy again. But today, just as she got to our door, she broke loose and bolted into our house with the policeman after her. She'd run around the table twice before they managed to catch her and take her out. After that, whenever we saw Nancy coming round the corner, we would dash in and shut the doors until the lark was once more put into its cage.

It wasn't only the children, however, who used to stand outside the

Station, just to hear how beautifully she sang. One day, when Mrs Lomas mentioned listening to Nancy Dickiebird, Mother said "Well, I think Nancy is more sinned against than sinning. She's probably got some good in her somewhere", and Mother was invariably right.

In those days, the Salvation Army Band were always somewhere about. The women in the Band weren't glamorous Beauty Queens, but they were dedicated to the cause. The men's uniforms were quite passable but the women's dresses were terribly dowdy. Long, full, shapeless skirts; black boots and stockings, and their hair parted in the middle, dragged back into a bun and finished off with a miserable little bonnet. But their hearts were in their work as they moved around, singing and shaking their tambourines.

One day, we were standing underneath Lily's window, playing "London Bridge is Falling Down" and we were singing quite loudly, when we heard music louder than ours. It was the Salvation Army Band. We broke from what we were doing and dashed to see the performance. The Band, with us kids joining in, were just singing "In the Sweet Bye and Bye" when one of my friends said "Hey, isn't that woman like Nancy Dickiebird?"

"Where," says I.

"Her, there at the end," she said.

"Ooh ay, she is, isn't she?" I said.

"It won't be her," said the other girl unconvincingly.

"It is her," we said, and we flew to tell our Mothers.

"Mam, Mam," I panted, "Nancy Dickiebird's joined the Salvation Army."

"Don't be daft," said Mother.

"Well, just you wait until they come around here, and you'll see." I said. Mother never even replied to the last remark, but went on with her knitting. She was making me some black woollen stockings on four needles. I went out again looking for my friends. I saw first one come out of the house and then the other. As we walked towards one another I said "did you tell your Mother?"

"Yes," said Ivy, "but she didn't believe me"

"My Mam didn't believe me either," said Lily.

The music stopped. After a while figures appeared with drum and tambourines, and Nancy!

"Man, Mam, now do you believe me?" I shouted. She came out of the house as did all our neighbours at the sound of any sort of music, and stared at the Sally Band. They couldn't believe their eyes, although they had heard Nancy sing before; they were amazed. I can't say I remember any tears, but Mother said afterwards that nearly everyone was crying at the sight of her.

As a child, I always had my bath, just like every other child, on a Friday night in a zinc bath in front of a lovely blazing coal fire. The kettle was always hot and always contained two small or one large iron pan full of water either for washing up, cleaning or for bath nights.

Mrs Lomas worked very hard for my Mother, washing the clothes, cleaning and looking after me, and she would always bath me on Friday nights. She'd have my clean vest and nightie on the steel stool by the fire and the towel warming on a nail at the side of the fire. She would wash my body with carbolic soap, and my hair with soft soap which made a lovely lather.

Friday night was also senna night. The stewed herb pod was used to keep your body in good condition and as a laxative, an 'opening' medicine. We were given senna as a matter of course, but if you had been complaining of belly-ache, you got a good large spoonful of thick, slimy castor oil as well if you were really lucky. You had the choice of the castor oil or a large spoonful of black treacle and sulphur, but before all this took place, Mother would take up the thick home-made rugs, should there be an accident.

After Mrs Lomas had finished with me, it would be Mother's turn to do her share - that would be some of the weekend cleaning. The black leading on the fireplace, and the steel fender, poker, tongs, and shovel belonging to it would all have to be cleaned. And if you accidentally splashed them with water you would have to spend ages scraping the rust off with emery paper. After you'd had your bath, the water would be put to good use. Nothing was wasted in those days. The first job involved scrubbing the table ready for baking on Sunday afternoon. Then, complete with "course" apron which was made of hessian, Mother would commence to kneel down and scrub the oilcloth on the floor, finishing off by the step at the front door. Then when all this was done, the water would be tipped down a grid outside.

She would refill her bucket and begin to clean the front window cill with whitestone, just like the step, then brownstone all the flags down to the curb. All this word had to be done on her hands and knees using soft soap before stoning. Everyone did the same, so by Saturday dinnertime, the long streets would look a picture.

Mother was able to see the "front" to clean it on Friday nights because everyone dressed their windows with long lace curtains which were usually made in Nottingham. The gas light with its mantle was usually on the wall at the side of the fireplace nearest the window and that

The Poultry Market on Shude Hill

threw a very good light outside through the open door. If you were passing these houses, you would be able to see everything inside, from aspidistra plants on the dresser to antimacassars on the back of the sofas and chairs. Framed photographs of Father as a little lad in Knickerbockers, with a large, stiff, flat, white collar and usually a pale face, would be going brown with age on the parlour wall, and a lot of the Catholic homes would have a large picture of the Pope or the Sacred Heart and the Virgin Mary opposite the window for the whole world to see. But the great favourite with everyone was the picture of the little child who had not noticed the broken plank in the little wooden bridge, being guided across by an angel. I wonder just what kind of a picture I made on full view on bath nights.

Saturday would be Mother's day for cleaning the backyard and entry, Everywhere would be swept first. Then the backyard grid, and the grid in the entry, would be cleaned with sheep dip. Everyone took that one in turns. The yard would be a lovely golden brown in the middle with a wide white band all round the side, a pattern we repeated in the entry.

We used to play in the yard quite a lot, for "house" or "shop" for instance, and the yard was used if your Mother wanted to keep the front door shut to keep the dog in when she was in season.

Although you could guarantee that three quarters of these doors, at any time of any day, would be either open or just 'put to' - on a Monday, these same doors didn't open until quite late in the day, usually towards tea-time. Then they'd be thrown open. All because the occupants hadn't wanted to see the landlord. Maybe they'd had a big "tick" bill at Mycocks and had been forced to pay it all. Maybe they'd had to pay the backlog because Mrs Mycock also had to pay her bills.

Of course, all the poverty wasn't genuine poverty. It was caused by the Fathers - and in some cases the Mothers - spending their money in pubs. They were always full with the sound of laughter; ragtime piano music and "boozy" choruses, until 'let-out' which was at eleven.

After the holidays were over, you would see the great migration to "Uncles" - the pawn shop. There would be a queue outside May's on Rochdale Road, long before the shop was open. Children and their mothers would be shivering in the cold, carrying large bundles wrapped in shawls or sheets. These would contain part of their bedding, and at home, a coat thrown over the bed would have to do.

Some women would only have a small inconspicuous bag with them. If you weren't in the queue with them, you wouldn't guess that they intended to pawn anything, but in the bag would probably be her husband's best brown boots.

Then there was the other woman who had no bag of any description. You would wonder why ever she stood in the queue. Then, as you moved up very slowly to the shop doorway, you'd realise why she's had you guessing. She'd work out her two arms from under her shawl and with her right hand, would slide off her wedding ring and pass it over the counter to one of the two or three assistants. You would hear her say "Can you give me a pound Mr May?" If she was a regular customer, she'd get the pound without any trouble, but if she wasn't a regular, he would weigh it on a dainty brass scale and make her an offer which she could take or leave.

And finally there was the other woman who would have her husband's best suit thrown tidily over her arm and covered with brown paper. This went on from Monday morning until Friday evening, and come Saturday, in uncomfortably hot sun or shivering cold, the week's borrowers would be waiting to pay their loan debt and receive their pledges.

Blankets and sheets would replace worn overcoats, Mrs White would wear her wedding ring, and Mr Green would be able to wear his brown boots and suit over the weekend before repeating the procedure on Monday.

A person had to work or starve in those days. There was no such thing as Social Security or the National Health Service. The equivalent of today's Department of Health and Social Security was called the Board of Guardians. You couldn't get anything free unless you bared your soul. As a result, many people came close to starving. Even the children of poor families were singled out as they handed in their 'green' ticket to get free meals, or collected their free pair of clogs. And come summer, many poor children had a welcome holiday, thanks to the Wood Street Mission on Deansgate. You'd no need to be desperately poor - coming from a poor neighbourhood would be sufficient for them to send you to St. Annes on Sea, but you had to be clean, with clean hair and clean underclothes. An examination took place a few days before the holiday, so if the children had any nits in their hair, they would use lamp oil and still have time to get rid of the smell before the great day arrived. If the lamp oil failed to work, the school officer in charge would get a pair of scissors and cut out all the offending hair, making them look right Charlies.

You must remember though, that the poverty which forced people to take holidays this way wasn't always as a result of the father's inability to carry out a full day's work, or hold down a steady job. Quite often, there wasn't the work for them to do. Those were the days of the slump, and a time when families had to rally together just pull through - and pull through we did.

Now, you will hear people say "Well, you could get a loaf for fourpence halfpenny and rent a house for about six to eight shillings, you should have been well-off", they don't realise one very important thing. There were no such things as holidays with pay. I wonder how some of today's men and women would have felt if, at Christmas, they were left without wages until after the holidays. How would they provide the Christmas food and toys for the children: the wages then for the whole week weren't half what people get for an hour today. Somehow, though, the children got something at Christmas, usually an orange and apple and a new penny in their stocking. Perhaps a "lucky bag" or a Christmas net stocking as their Christmas bundle.

CHAPTER 6

Aunty Betsy Carter

I wasn't very well acquainted with Aunt Betsy Carter: I had visited her a few times but I thought she was very severe-looking, and she made so much of a fuss of me last time I went. So I didn't care for her too much and showed little interest in the increasing number of conversations in which her name was mentioned.

The only auntie I was well acquainted with was Aunt Ellen, my Great Aunt who was actually my Mother's Mother's Sister. Mother just called her Aunt Ellen and her husband was Uncle Frank Feasey. I thought she was a beautiful cook, far nicer than my Mother or Mrs Lomas, and I used to go every Sunday morning without fail for dinner at her house in Abbott Street right opposite Abbott Street School.

She used to put my dinner plate on a stool in the lobby and that was where I had my meal, which incidentally I always thoroughly enjoyed. Especially the tapioca pudding and blackcurrant jam which I used to mix up until it went pink. And Uncle Frank never forgot to give me my Sunday penny which I would spend on an everlasting stick from from the toffee shop opposite Piggie Riley's pawnshop.

One day, her little dog Nellie knocked my pudding all over the lobby floor. Aunt Ellen had to leave her dinner and come to clean it up before it was spread all over the house. When I told my Mother about Nellie and my dinner, my Mother asked

"What were you doing in the lobby?"

"Having my dinner," I said

"I know that, I mean why does she put you there?"

"She always puts me there," I said "She said I might dirty the table-cloth".

"Her and her table-cloths and antimacassars on everything. She'd go insane if you sat on her seven piece suite without the covers on. Her dirty tablecloths are as clean as when she's washed, and ironed them," Mother stormed. She didn't understand that I didn't mind eating in the lobby and in spite of everything, I liked Aunt Ellen. She was a fat lady; she weighed eighteen stones and as she walked, she rocked from side to side. She didn't go out much, only to the corner shop or to visit the Cinema picture house at the top of Dalton Street, opposite Reather

Street. Nellie, her dog, used to belong to us when we were in Buxton. The day my Dad bought me my yellow clogs and Tam O'Shanter, he also brought me this little pup. I remember he came in a pony and trap with the man who owned it and an elderly gentleman who was a cobbler from Stockport by the name of Bob Cream.

I loved little Nellie because she was so active and so full of fun. She was in fact too full of fun, and she caused terrible furores with the ladies in Buxton. They didn't wear clogs and shawls; they wore the most gorgeous lacy hats and beautiful dresses with flounces on them. These "ladies" were most evident in summer when they filled the many hotels.

In those days there was very little traffic, so Mother used to let Nellie out to run around. One day she was getting ready to take me out. I was sitting on the table washing my legs, when outside we heard a bit of a commotion. We glanced towards the window, through which we could see the top half of two ladies, one frantically wielding a lovely frilly parasol.

"I think it's Nellie," said Mother. "What's she doing?"

"Is she hitting her with her umbrella?" I cried with horror.

"Wait a minute - stay there," said Mother, making for the door. Almost the moment Mother got there, she shouted sternly "Nellie, Nellie, come here!"

Those were the days before I obeyed anyone, and although Mother had told me to sit still, I promptly got down just in time to hear the lady say "Is this your horrible little dog? Just look at my dress!" There she was, standing with the flounce of her dress almost completely torn off. Nellie had chased both of the ladies, playing with the floppy frills of their dresses. Mother was terrified and offered to repair the dress by hand, but the lady said she would want it mending by the dressmaker who had made it, and that Mother would receive the bill. This worried Mother, but fortunately for us, that was the last we heard of it.

Around that time, we had a new rag and bone man. In those days you gave rags which were re-pulped, bones which were made into glue, and bottles which the man re-sold. You got balloons galore if you had plenty of rags; after a visit by the rag and bone man all the children in the street had a balloon.

This particular man also had a nice collection of cups and saucers, dinner and tea plates, fruit bowls and a variety of things which you could exchange proving you had enough rags. He'd move down the street, shouting "Pots for old rags - Pots for old rags", and of course, he always had the old traditional rubbing stones. Brown ones, white ones, hard fawn donkey stones, and blue stones for the hearth.

One day, Mother sorted out everything she could find; things that I had outgrown and oddments from Mrs Lomas, including an old feather boa. She put everything in a basket at the door which was well back from the road, and as it was a windy day, Mother laid two bottles on the top to prevent everything blowing out.

Because of the trouble Nellie caused that Day, Dad had issued orders that she had only to go out on a lead or stay inside with me. We were busy playing when Mrs Parr called. Mother opened the door, and out dashed Nellie.

"Come here Nellie, come here Nellie," cried Mother. "I hope she's not doing any damage."

"I don't think so," said Mrs Parr. "There's no-one about on a day like this."

That remark seemed to satisfy Mother who thanked Mrs Parr for the Red Letter paper she had brought, and went indoors.

"I hope Nellie comes home before we go to the chemist," Mother said.

Nellie didn't return and we were ready for going out, when we heard the hooves of the horse, and the wheels of the cart, and the voice of the Rag and Bone Man shouting "Pots for old Rags." He was slowly coming down the street and would knock when he saw the basket.

Mother was still worried that Nellie hadn't returned, and was about to look out of the door when the man knocked. As soon as she opened the door, he greeted her with "Aye, those must have been your rags that are blowing up Fairfield Road. There's a wild little dog running around with a fur round its neck. There's drawers (meaning my knickers) and all sorts blowing around. It's too windy to go chasing after them." Mother was very annoyed.

"I've been saving up for six china cups and saucers." said Mother.

"Well I haven't any china left anyway, but I'll tell you what I'll do. Next week I'll bring your cups and saucers and you can find me a bit at a time. "Mother thanked him and he found a balloon in his box for me, which Mother fastened to a stick. As she handed it to me she made it quite clear that the least Dad knew about Nellie and her knavish tricks the better. So neither of us mentioned a thing about it, and my father, who was working as a porter at The Royal Hotel in Buxton was none the wiser.

One day we went an errand and arrived back home with Dad's ointment, and there was Nellie crying to get in. She didn't see us until Mother called "Where do you think you've been, you little divil?" Nellie dashed to us and jumped up to me. "Get down you naughty girl." said Mother, giving her a little push.

"Don't hit her, she' only a baby." I cried.
"Yes, well, I have enough with you, without having to cope with a disobedient dog." I shut my mouth.

Anyway, after Nellie's next performance, which was chasing the hens and chickens next door, Dad decided that she had to go. We'd heard Aunt Ellen wanted a dog, so Nellie got a new owner and eventually learned to behave and be sensible.

I knew that I loved Aunt Ellen and Uncle Frank, but I was very undecided about Great Aunt Betsy. Her name was mentioned again that day, and I became more curious. I thought I'd try and get the gist of the conversation next time I heard her name mentioned.

This happened as I came in from school. My Dad was ready to go out, dressed in his best navy blue Sunday suit.

"Where are you going?" I asked.
"To Great Aunt Betsy's" he replied.
"What for?"
"She's not very well."
"I don't think I like Great Aunt Betsy," I said.
"You'd better learn to then, we're going to live with her."

Live with her! I was stunned and numbed. I'd have to leave my special friends, and Dickie Banks, and Sonny, his son who sat with us, not to mention the Mission, the Wakes and the 'Hip'. There was the Park, and there was Mrs Lomas. What would I do without her? Who would be there to give me my cocoa and sugar, or oatmeal and sugar to take to school for playtime. Who would meet me with a butty of full-cream condensed milk whilst I waited for tea-time?

I felt like playing wag! I wouldn't be able to earn the odd ha'penny going with Ivy for coal for fat Mrs Mason and her very thin sister-in-law Mrs Hamilton.

I was dead miserable.

Friday night meant bathtime once. again. As there was no school the following day, I looked forward to going to Dickie's as usual. Or at least, I thought so..... my parents had other ideas.

"I'll put your hair in rags tomorrow night," said Mrs Lomas.
"Why?" I asked.
"For Great Aunt Betsy's on Sunday."

I was very quiet. My Dad was reading the 'John Bull' and my mother was 'trying a cake' with a big hat-pin which was about seven inches long. If there was cake stuck on the pin when she pulled it out, then it wasn't cooked. If the pin was clean and dry, it was.

"I don't want to go," I whispered very softly to Mrs Lomas.

40   SUNRISE TO SUNSET

I'm certain Dad didn't hear, but being my Dad, he didn't need to hear. He just said "No whispering," and I knew quite definitely that he knew exactly what I'd whispered. My Dad knew everything - I swear he heard the sun setting.

Mrs Lomas tried to comfort me by saying very softly "You're going for some new shoes tomorrow, you'll like that, won't you?" If the shoes had been for any other occasion other than going to Great Aunty Betsy's, maybe I wouldn't have minded forfeiting something. But to forfeit Dickie Banks's was too much. I was following a serial there. The Indians had surrounded the stage-coach and had shot the driver, but the Mounties were on their way and the Indians didn't know. This week would see the battle between the goodies and the baddies. Mind you, I didn't need to know what happened, the poor old Indians lost every time.

Mother had decided to do her baking tonight to give her time to go out to town the next day for my shoes. Her next job was the cleaning, and so I went to bed.

The following morning we had a lie-in, and set off for the shops after breakfast.

We'd never gone so early before. We arrived in town and got off the tram and went to Freeman Hardy & Willis, where we bought a pair of black patent, silver-buckled shoes. From there we went to the cookshop in a side street just off Tib Street. There were one or two similar shops in the city centre. They had the largest potato, or meat, or rabbit pies that you've ever seen in your whole life. They were placed in three very large holes in a sort of counter which was right beneath the window. They were kept hot by using steam from underneath, which at times, escaped out around the pies. The pies were about twenty-four inches across, and the potato or meat pies contained tons of lovely onions and carrots, as well as the lashings of meat, and you would be spoiled for choice because the rabbit pie was lovely too. If you wanted a dinner of mashed potatoes, veg and rabbit, it would cost you about three pennies, and for that you'd get a front leg. If you had a back leg, then this would cost you a copper more. You could get a plate of the potato or meat pie for 3d or 4d. If you didn't want a dinner, you could buy a plate of black peas, and a penny for the bread, and a lovely strong hot cup of tea would be another penny.

After a visit to Shudehill market, we arrived home in time for tea.

We were just going into the house when we heard the call of a man's voice. "Hush," said Mother, "I think I heard the Crumpet Man". Sure enough, we heard "Crumpets and pikelets, two a penny." Crumpets and

Flat Iron Market

pikelets, two a penny." "Go and get eight," said Mother putting four pennies in my hand.

As we tucked into the crumpets, Mother reminded me about my hair. I was ready for bed, but not very thrilled at having to suffer tortures all night with my hair rags. Mother wanted to make a good impression on Great Aunt Betsy and wanted to show me off by taking me to see her with ringlets in my hair. The result might have looked nice, but putting hair rags in was a right process which involved wrapping your hair, in strands, round a long rag. When it was all finished and your head was covered,you looked like a handful of sore fingers. Fortunately, to undo this was much, much easier. All that was needed was to undo the knot in the middle, gently unwrap the rag from the bottom, then from the top, then pull the whole rag downwards through the centre of the curl. The result was a lovely head of long, gorgeous curls: just the thing for Great Aunt Betsy.

CHAPTER 7

To Angel Meadow

It was Sunday and the day we were to visit Aunt Betsy's.

I don't ever remember my Parents attending Mass regularly, but Mrs Lomas was very keen on taking me to Church and making sure that I went to Confession.

After Mass that morning, we had a lovely dinner of lamb, roast potatoes and vegetables, and after dinner we set off to Aunty Betsy's. As it was a nice day, we walked - round into North Kent Street, into Collyhurst Street, past the Prince of Wales pub, round Slater's corner and on to Rochdale Road. We passed the chemist on the corner where Mam bought her carmine, the senna pods and Mrs Lomas's mustard plaster for her back pains.

Then we came to May's Pawnshop where my Mam and Dad stood looking at the forfeited pledges for sale in the window. All the rings, bangles, watches and earrings, each telling the tale of the owner who pawned them because they were hard up, and then became too poor to ever redeem them.

Further on we reached another pawnshop by the name of Piggie Riley's which had a large aspidistra in the middle of the window. Next we had to pass the urinal where men went in undoing their trousers and came out again fastening them up. The smell was enough to knock you over - and it lingered with us as we turned into Reather Street where Aunt Ellen lived.

We decided to call in and as we got to Aunt Ellen's, we noticed that the house next door was empty and had a big notice in the window which said; TO LET: Key next door.

Mother was surprised to hear that the owner, a lovely old lady, had died and that it was her aspidistra in the pawnshop window. The landlord was now looking for a new tenant and was asking for four shillings for the first week's rent.

After our brief visit, we set off again on our journey to Aunty Betsy's. As we crossed the road we passed a house with the name 'Stiles' over the door. Mam said this was the undertaker used by all the Catholics for miles around.

We passed Thomson Street Goods yard where, as it was Sunday, the

The children of the Ragged School waiting outside the school in Ashley Lane, Angel Meadow.

trains and waggons stood on the tram lines in the middle of the road, past the Victoria Inn and the Marble Arch pub, the Baptist Chapel and a cook shop identical to the one in the Market and before we knew it, we were in Angel Meadow and Great Aunt Betsy's.

Aunt Betsy had three houses. One in Angel Street, and the other two, which were next to each other, round the corner in St. Michael's Square which is the part of Angel Meadow on all the old photographs of the area.

We knocked at the door of her little house which was on the corner opposite the church. Aunty Betsy who was dressed all in black and wearing gold earrings, opened the door and smiled. She looked straight at me and said "Well, you do look nice;" that not only surprised me but delighted me too, and she continued by asking Mother where she had bought my shoes, saying too that she like my hair. How satisfying!

They started talking about a Solicitor and things that didn't much interest me, so I went playing with Fanny, a ginger-coloured Airedale dog who was old and going blind, and Bulla the cat, who must have been neutered he was such a weight. I nursed the cat and stroked the dog until they called me for my tea, which was salmon and salad. The business must have been finished, because as soon as we finished our tea, we caught the tram home.

Mrs Lomas was out when we arrived home, she hadn't come back from Benediction, so one of the first things Mother did after taking off my Sunday clothes was to clean my clogs for school on Monday morning. I was tired and falling asleep, and offered no resistance when Mam took me up the dancers - which was our name for the stairs - to bed. No sooner was I tucked in than I fell fast asleep.

Mrs Lomas went first thing on Monday for the plant at Piggy's. The aspidistra, complete with a fancy plantpot painted with birds and leaves without branches was placed very convincingly on the dresser. I'm afraid I didn't like it; it was all leaves and drowned everything else. I would have preferred something small and pretty and told Mrs Lomas so. She replied that I wouldn't have to put up with it much longer, as we were going to live with Great Aunty Betsy in Angel Meadow, or to give it it's posh title, "St. Michael's Square".

However, it was many weeks before we actually moved, but we did visit a few times and I came to like Great Aunty Betsy more and more.

Dad was doing a lot of errands for her, something about the Solicitor amongst other things, and one day, when he came in, Mother asked "Is that the last?"

"Yes," he answered, "You know, I feel rotten about this; I'm not keen at all. The only thing is, I'll be able to give up my job." I didn't know what he meant until weeks after.

In addition to all this, it seemed that we were going to have a lodger - "Young Eva", the daughter of Mrs Lomas. As we were leaving, it seems Eva was going to give up her job as a waitress in Buxton, and come to live with her Mother in our old house. She would be company for her, and would help with the household bills. She was coming on Saturday and because of the shortage of space, she was to sleep in my bed whilst I was to share with her Mother. We'd only two bedrooms; my Parents had the front one and normally Mrs Lomas and myself were in two separate single beds in the back room which faced the back windows of North Kent Street.

As soon as Eva arrived I was captivated by her.

I had helped her to unpack and she had given me some real tortoiseshell beads and hairslides. But the article which attracted my attention was little box with lovely pearl drops, which reminded me of tears, on it. "What's in the box, Eva," I asked. She reluctantly opened the box, taking out a handful of letters.

"They're my love letters," she replied, "from my young man, Phil," I immediately wanted to know more about Phil and over the next few weeks, I had the chance to meet him. Four times a week I would check if Phil was waiting for Eva at their arranged meeting place under

Mycocks window. Eva needn't have worried - Phil was always there, and for the errand, he gave me a halfpenny. Soon he was accepted by everyone, including Dad, and he was given permission to knock. Dad didn't mind, so long as the table had been cleared and the pots put into the slopstone at the back, and fortunately, I didn't loose my halfpenny; he gave to me just the same.

Those were some of my happiest times. I rarely got into trouble and Dad was always talking to me, answering my questions and helping me to understand the things which were going on around me. But there was one question which would always bring the same two answers. "When we save enough money" from my parents, and "When God thinks the time is right" from Mrs Lomas.

The question was "When can we have another baby?"

The day of final settlement arrived and we prepared to move. It seems that we were leaving everything except my garf, bobbers and kibs, shuttlecock and paddle, whip and top, skipping ropes, slate and slate pencil, and my piggy and stick - not forgetting my Mr Kelly's which were in a tin box. I had about twenty of them all brought by my Grandfather. I think Dad had given all the contents of the house to Mrs Lomas; I couldn't imagine him wanting to be paid for things he didn't need.

But there was one thing I wanted, but I was afraid to ask him for. That was the picture of the Angel guiding the child over the broken bridge. It was one of the first pictures mother had bought from a second-hand shop in Buxton and it had always had pride of place over the old red sofa opposite the window.

Dad had arranged for the rag man to bring his cart and little donkey to move our boxes of clothes. Emma, the donkey, was very docile and whilst Dad was making sure everything was going well, I was feeding her with carrots and crusts. It was six o'clock after tea on Saturday. The man had wanted to do the job on Sunday morning, but Great Aunt Betsy nearly had hysterics. She didn't want atheists coming into her house on a Sunday. The very idea - to do a removal job on the Lord's Day! It was sacrilege, so the rag-bone man had to come on Saturday night and miss his night out in the Osborne House pub at the corner of Osborne Street and Rochdale Road.

Everything was ready for the off. Dad and I got on the cart and sat on a blanket. Mother was going to go down by tram, so she, Mrs Lomas, and Eva waved us off. I had tears in my eyes at the thought of leaving Eva, and Mrs Lomas had tears in her eyes because she was losing me. All my friends, Ivy and Lily, Tommy Lamb and Sister Nellie, and all the neighbours were out to wave us off. I felt very upset especially at the

Donkey carts were often in use in this period, and were common in Manchester up to the First World War.

thought of leaving the picture which I could just see through the lace curtains.

"Cheer up, you'll soon get used to Aunt Betsy, she's not so bad," my Dad said.

"It's not that," I replied.

"Oh, is it Ivy and Lily and Tommy Lamb," he said, adding with a smile, "and Tommy Mycock?" He even knew that I had a crush on little Tommy Mycock.

"No, it's the picture," I said.

"What picture?"

"That one there," I said, pointing to the Angel.

"Well, you could have had it if you'd asked before," he said. "We've given it to Mrs Lomas now."

He got down from the front of the cart, and went slowly to the door where Mrs Lomas was standing. He spoke to her and they both turned, passed Mother and Eva and went inside where I could see them unhooking the picture from the wall.

They seemed to be looking around them, then Mrs Lomas bent down, picked up the hand-brush out of the blue stoned hearth and brushed the dust from behind the picture into the hob in front of the fire. Dad handed the picture to me and we slowly moved off on the road to Travellers Call in Angel Meadow, and a more adventurous life than I could ever have imagined.

CHAPTER 8

Traveller's Call

Emma the donkey, who'd pulled the removal cart for us, was glad to trot off home after being out all day. People, unintentionally, were rather cruel to donkeys in those days. The donkeys would be very well fed, but they were given especially heavy weights to pull on their carts. They were treated like ants who can pull many times their own weight, but they never went short of food. They would always be seen with their hay bags around their necks and there was always someone who would bring out a bowl of water for them, so I suppose they were happy. Emma was a typical girl. She had a bit of ribbon in her hair and lots of brasses down her back and was always looking for attention. If she was left alone, she would start bellowing "Hee-Haw", a call which always attracted the children or women of the neighbourhood. The women all fell for the call, especially on a Monday morning when there might be some bits of cake or pie over from tea the day before.

Emma had gone now and we had gone into Aunt Betsy's house. She had the most gorgeous home. China, glassware, hand-crochet antimacassars; lovely brass fire-irons with a very long shovel, coal tongs through the fender at one side of the fire, and poker at the other. There was a brass pedestal-type stool with a copper kettle standing on top, which was boiling madly, the lid clattering with the steam and dancing up and down frantically. Aunt Betsy brewed the tea.

"Do you want a drink of tea, Jim?" she asked, "And do you want some pop, Mary?"

"Yes please," I answered.

Aunt Betsy brought me a small stone bottle with "Ginger Beer" printed on it. Fanny the dog, remembering me from my last visit, moved from her position on the very colourful pegged rug in front of a huge roaring fire and rubbed herself against me so that I would stroke her as I had done last time.

We hadn't been in the house long when someone knocked on the door. "This'll be Polly," said Dad. It was indeed my Mother with her two bags of bits and pieces - one bag containing her hair pads, tortoiseshell hair-slides, hair-pins and small curling tongs along with two button hooks for our boots - a small one for me and larger one with a pearl handle. I remember the lovely little lace collar which she laid out reverently on the table. Mrs Lomas had crocheted it for me for Sundays and had only finished it that evening in time for my Mother to bring it with her to our new address.

Mother's other bag contained mostly books. Her main hobby was reading very good educational books, although it never got her anywhere in life. I helped her get them out of her bag, gazing at the titles as we unpacked them. Thee was a book of plays, one called "The Bondsman", another "The Sign of the Cross". There were pictures of Mrs Patrick Campbell, Henry Ainley, and a lady named Terry.

I remember the lovely postcard photographs of the lady in "The Sign of the Cross". She'd got beautiful long, wavy hair down to her waist, and she wore a Greek-style high-busted dress with a girdle around the waist. There were six postcards of different poses of the lady in different parts of the play, but the one which really took my eye was the one with the words underneath which said,

"Is it her faith makes her so beautiful. Or does she beautify her faith?"

I was nine years old when I first took any interest in this book, but it put me on the road to develop an intense pleasure from very good books for the rest of my life. I had been an exceptionally good reader from first starting school, and so I got very deeply engrossed in this book - until Aunt Betsy turned around and saw me, exclaiming almost in horror, "Polly, have you seen what she's reading?"

Mother immediately took the book from me and put in in a bookcase

In Angel Meadow and St. Chad's, Cheetham Hill.

where the key was always left in the hole. Needless to say, that didn't present any problems and because of all the excitement, I read all the plays and two other besides, one a tragedy and one an opera. It seems my Mother bought these lovely books from a second-hand book stall in Shudehill hen market.

Of course, arriving in a new neighbourhood meant that I'd have no friends and I would probably have to wait until I started at St. Chad's Catholic School, Lord Street, the following Monday morning. The evening passed quickly and soon we went upstairs to bed, leaving Aunt Betsy Carter to sleep downstairs in her large double bed with valances all round the bottom, and curtains made of snow white linen all the way round the sides and top. Underneath was the chamber pot which was white with big blue flowers all around the outside mingled with gold leaves, a leaf finishing off the handle.

Next morning, being Sunday, I got up and went to Mass at St. William's Church in Simpson Street. On my way out of church, I was dumbfounded when I realised that I was coming out of Mass with someone I knew very well. It was Madelaine! Not only that, but she was living next door to us.

"What are you doing in St. Williams?" I asked her.

"Well, we've come to live at the bottom of Angel Meadow," she said.

"Well, we've come to live with Great Aunt Betsy in Saint Michael's Square round your corner," I said, "at Travellers Call."

"Oh, is Mrs Carter your Auntie?" asked Madelaine.

"Well, she likes to be called Great Aunt Betsy."

"Oh, heck," laughed Madelaine.

Aunt Betsy didn't get up very early next morning, She waited until my Mother took her a drink of tea. She didn't want anything to eat. Mother remarked to Dad that in her opinion, Aunt Betsy didn't look very well.

"Do you think she needs the doctor?" asked Dad.

"No, I don't think so; anyway it's Sunday," Mother replied.

"Doctor won't bother about that," said Dad, which was quite true in those days. Doctors would turn out any hour of the day or night for weeks on end and then pay a man to collect the bill - which was often paid at the rate of sixpence a week. Many patients never paid, they simply couldn't afford it.

Besides Madelaine I also found other friends - one was Rosie Ann, there was also Emily and two Polish friends, Mary and Julia, as well as Julia's sister Annie.

Later, I met another Polish friend named Hannah. But I only met her going to and from school. Her Mother wouldn't let her play near Angel

Meadow. She thought, like a lot of others, that only rogues, thieves and vagabonds lived there. Which of course was absolutely ridiculous.

As the weeks passed by, Aunt Betsy didn't seem to be getting any better - she'd get up late and go to bed early, and I was beginning to realise how cramped we were getting, spending most of the time with Aunty Betsy in her combined room. I wanted to go into the other two houses which also belonged to her, and where I could hear people talking and laughing but my Dad wouldn't let me go in. He or Mother would go in occasionally, "Just to see how things were".

I was given the job of being errand girl for the first couple of weeks. My favourite errand was to go to Peter's Cellar at the corner of Dantzic Street and Crown Square. It was only a little lock-up shop but he sold groceries, and toffees; everlasting sticks, for a farthing, bullseyes, scented hearts and all sorts. He was a very jovial man, very dark and spotlessly clean with a nice laundered starched apron over his ample tummy.

After we'd been in Angel Meadow for about a month, I was woken up one morning for school by my Dad which was unusual, it was mostly Mother's job.

"Get up Mary, your Mother's gone to Aunt Theresa Ellen's" Dad said.

"What for?"

"Well, she's gone for the doctor and Aunt Theresa Ellen because Great Aunt Betsy's dead. She died in her sleep. Aunt Theresa Ellen knows how to wash her and lay her out." This to me was a completely new experience.

Aunt Betsy was duly laid out. A white corpse in an all-white bed, until the doctor had been and Mr Stiles had measured her for her coffin. My Father, I suppose must have been responsible for the funeral arrangements, even though Aunt Betsy had a son. Of course, I didn't know about funeral arrangements. I wasn't interest in that, but I've got the most vivid memories of Great Aunt Betsy's death.

Although she was the first corpse I'd seen, apart from the baby, I wasn't in the least bit afraid of being on my own with her. As a child, and all through my adult life, I have never been a nervous or frightened person.

The Undertaker had been and laid Aunt Betsy out in the coffin - a good expensive oak one. It was put on trestles, with tall candlesticks which came from the floor, to above the coffin. The Undertaker had put her hands together as if in prayer, and wrapped her rosary beads around her fingers.

I remember quite plainly the first night she was put in her coffin. Mother and Father didn't want to go to bed leaving Aunt Betsy on her own all night. They believed in the old tradition of having a wake for the dead and staying up all night. Although my parents weren't churchgoers, they were very superstitious about a lot of things their parents had told them, so they covered up all the mirrors and said the rosary.

I didn't understand all this.

Before all this wakes business started though, my parents told me that they would be going into Aunt Betsy's bed later during the night as, apart from leaving Aunt Betsy, they were afraid of the candles catching alight, and with Bulla the cat rambling all over the place, this was quite likely.

On realising that I would have to go to bed alone, I said "Can I sleep on the sofa, I don't want to sleep on my own upstairs?"

"Why, are you frightened?" asked my Mother.

"No, but I don't like that horrible room upstairs," I said.

Dad said, "It's going to mean you losing your sleep. Your Mother and I have got to attend to the houses. We'll have to go and talk to the people before we settle down, and it's eight o'clock now. You won't want to lie on the sofa, the coffin's next to it, and you'll be on your own."

"I'm not frightened, it's very bright," I said, "there's the light from the candles."

"All right then, but be very careful you don't catch the candles when you're getting undressed," said Dad again.

I got undressed and Mother tucked me in the best she could, which was awkward really, as there were no cushions to tuck the bedding under. When she had finished, she looked down at me and said "I'll bet you don't sleep."

They both left me to go into the other houses which were only a door away. I could see the gas light shining from under the door, and I could hear the voices of the people, even though the door was closed to stop Fanny from wandering.

From where I was lying on the sofa, I could just see the tip of Aunt Betsy's nose and her fingers clutching the rosary. The yellow golden gleam of the candles fascinated me as I gently blew them to see if I could get them to all go in the same direction at exactly the same time. Finally, I fell asleep, but woke up during the night because the bedclothes had fallen off me, and I was feeling cold. Being an unspoilt child, I didn't disturb my parents, but got off the sofa and tried to make my bed, which was very awkward, a small child trying to handle large sheets and blankets. I was struggling, when I heard a voice say, "What are you doing?" I was startled at first, thinking it was Aunt Betsy, because I was thinking to myself, "Mind the coffin, don't knock Aunt Betsy over." I looked at the clock; it said twenty minutes past four; I was terrified. The voice bellowed out again - it was my Mother. She came over to me and covered me over for the second time, and we all went back to sleep again.

The next day I went to school as usual and brought in three of my friends at dinner time to "Have a look" at Aunt Betsy. They knelt down and said "Hail, Mary" and then went home for their meal. Whilst Mother and I were having our dinner, someone knocked on the dividing door. It was "Big Lizzie" - could she "Have a look" at Aunty Betsy? Mother let her in and gave her a tot of whisky, having bought a bottle just for this purpose - for people offering their condolences. Lizzie knelt down, said a prayer, inquired about the funeral and left.

This sort of thing went on for almost a full week. People coming and praying, having a little "tot" and going home. No-one was ever in a hurry to bury their dead. There was such a lot to be done anyway - insurance, undertakers...... But, the thing that took the most time, was the shopping for mourning black. Everyone close to the deceased would be completely in black; shoes, stockings, coats, gloves and hats for the ladies, and black suits for the men. Secondary mourning attire would be dark grey with black silk band around the arm. This black clothing would be worn for a full twelve months after the funeral by the near relatives.

Aunty Betsy had been dead for about six days before we buried her. Each day the smell of death got stronger, although the window was open. After many more visitors (who made it obvious that they were fond of the spirits in more ways than one) and more "Hail Marys" and "Our Fathers", Aunt Betsy was carried off to Moston Cemetery by the pale-faced undertaker and four carriers with their top hats, black suits, and each with a tot of whisky in their tummies. The gorgeous black and chestnut horses were beautifully groomed by Mr Stiles the undertaker himself, their heads nodding slowly as though they were saying "Yes, yes, that's the end of Great Aunt Betsy Carter, R.I.P."

All the people in our houses had given towards a large wreath, the collection being organised by Priscilla who had lived for years with Great Aunty Betsy. She got sixpences from the regulars, and pennies and twopences from the others. Mother and I went to the florist in the market in Swan Street and ordered ours. They were delivered the morning of the funeral and placed side by side on one of the long tables in the living kitchen. Mother wrote the card out for the lodgers; they expressed their sentiments in their own way, even though the words were not grammatically correct. They read "Sadly missed by all who have known Mrs Carter by living under the same roof."

Ours was just "Sadly missed by Jim, Polly and Mary".

CHAPTER 9

The Little Tin Box

The funeral over and paid for, Mother's first job was to try and collect all Great Aunt Betsy's clothes from the drawers of the chiffonier, so as to make room for our meagre oddments. Aunt Betsy had several heavy dresses, all with beads on the bust and high necks, which were made stiff by a couple of small pieces of whale-bone at the sides. There were several shawls, just for the shoulder, and all in different colours, and underskirts, stays and drawers in every cupboard.

Her winter drawers were made of either cream or red flannel whilst her summer ones were of white calico. Mother found four and a half pairs of calico ones, because one "pair" only consisted of one leg on a band with one tape instead of two legs with a tape at each end. They'd been returned from the laundry like this. Mother asked "Scotch Esther" a lodger about them, to be told that Aunt Betsy had written to the laundry responsible for the mishap, only to be told that one of the legs had got fast in the calender, and if they came across the other leg, they would send it or compensate, but Esther hadn't heard the outcome of the lost leg -

"Chase me Jimmy, I've lost me shimmy,
And half the leg of my drawers" she sang
Maybe she'd joined the "Odd Fellows" laughed Dad.

The dresses were too large for my Mother as she was a small dainty person, but the heaps of black cashmere stockings and drawers came in very useful. My Mother also kept the shawls.

Aunt Maggie, Mother's eldest sister, and Mother took all the best clothes to a dealer, but the old combinations, which were woollen, all-in-one, long-legged and long-sleeved undergarments, and the calico shifts were taken by Aunt Theresa Ellen and sold to a man on the Flat Iron Market, which was only five minutes or less away from my Great Grandfather's house in Marsden Court, off Fennell Street.

Although I realised that had Great Aunt Betsy lived, I could have loved her very much, I still felt awfully guilty because sorting out her clothes, I was really having the most marvellous experience I had ever had, or was ever likely to have in my whole life. This experience, I think, gave me the urge all through my adult life to go to as many jumble

15-23 Crown Lane — Angel Meadow.

sales as I could manage, buying many things which I could not have bought otherwise.

In one corner of the fireplace at the left hand side was a large let-in narrow cupboard with drawers at the bottom. Mother decided to take out the drawers and wash them after we had emptied them. I was doing the emptying and Mother doing the washing part. There were beautiful real pearl buttons, gorgeous bone, silver, and genuine leather covered shoe buckles, which even then must have been very old - Mother said that they had belonged to "young shoes", meaning Aunt Betsy when she was girl.

There was a lovely old lace collar; hand-made by deft delicate fingers. Its pattern consisted of ivory satin flowers about one inch across, and each flower was edged with an almost invisible piping so that they didn't fray. After each separate flower, leaf and stalk were piped, they were joined together into a pattern by the most delicate of cottons - the cotton stitching being in a pattern of its own. This really was the beginning of my appreciation of beautiful things.

Although I thought that I had got the most beautiful collar in existence when I got Mrs Lomas's hand-crocheted one, this one really was something, especially as Mother pointed out Aunt Betsy wearing the collar as a lovely young woman on a photograph on the mantelpiece.

During my job of "Mother's help" and being carried away with thoughts of treasure troves, I heard a gasp from Mother. Thinking immediately that she had decided to take up Dad's role by remonstrating at my lack of co-operation, I turned around to see the last full drawer on the floor and Mother holding an old tin box, her eyes popping out of her head.

"What is it Mam?" I asked

"Nothing." she said, very quickly, at the same time clamping the lid back on the box and putting in on the back of the chiffonier. By the look of her face I knew that there was something out of the ordinary because she had the same pale look as she had when I had been lost. Was the box full of Hairy Marys, I wondered.

"Don't you dare touch that box," said Mother after a couple of minutes. "And hurry up and empty that drawer before your Dad comes back from the 'stone shop'", meaning a little shop behind the Weaver's Arms where the lady sold sand for the floors, blue-stone for the hearthstone and white and brown donkey-stones for the fronts.

She kept looking through the lace curtains as though on pins. I knew that she was looking for my Dad, but as we were in an end-house and Dad had to come around the corner, she couldn't see him until he almost put his foot on the step, but she still looked. "Anyway," I thought, "I'll have another root and listen in when Dad comes in". Eventually, Dad came back with the sand barrel under his arm.

Before he had time to put the barrel down, Mother met him with "Eh, Jim, just look here," and at the same time lifting up the box.

"What is it?" he asked.

"Look," she said, handing him the box, but at the same time placing him with his back to me, which I took to mean "Your presence is not needed."

"Where did you find them?" he asked.

"On the floor beneath the bottom drawer over there," said Mam.

"They must be worth a pretty penny," said Dad.

"Well, I thought we'd got a fortune getting these," said Mam, fingering her mounted gold half sovereign earrings, and the three sovereigns on a bar, as a brooch on her neck. But still they wouldn't tell me what the box contained. And the contents remained a mystery to me until much later in my life.

All drawers emptied, cleaned and put back, I was told to wash my hands whilst Mother swept the rubbish from the oilcloth floor. All the things I wanted to keep I put back in the bottom drawer. The mystery box had disappeared, and soon I forgot all about it as Dad was not letting me go into Aunt Betsy's other houses. People were sitting around with mostly happy faces. The big thing missing, though, was drink; that, and swearing, being against the rule. My Father brought everyone's attention to the Notice on the wall which read:

"No foul language or the intake of alcohol in any shape or form allowed on these premises" (Signed) Mrs Carter.

We now had two houses besides our little private house on the corner. I had a little bedroom of my own which I could lock, and it was cosy; unlike the other which looked onto the side of Baxendale's Warehouse.

Mam and Dad, like Aunty Betsy Carter, used to sleep downstairs.

I was still asking the same old question, "When can we have a baby?" and still I got the old reply, "When we've enough money." This puzzled me, because I remembered last time we had a baby, both my parents had to go to work to buy its clothes and bassinette. Now, neither of my parents went to work. Was this what he meant when he'd said one day to my Mother that he'd be able to give up his job? Things were coming into focus now. I went to bed with a very happy little mind, but unfortunately I had an annoying little "tug" in my gum. I had a tooth going bad.

Next morning, I looked through the window, Madelaine in a red gansy and plaid kilt was going to school, She, and her cousins, were the "swanks" of the district. They were all noted for their good looks and exceptionally beautiful teeth. My tooth next morning was giving me gyp. Dad didn't believe in me staying off school, so not being a marred child, I didn't say anything to anyone, called for Annie my little Polish friend who lived at Scotland, a little street of railinged houses on the bank of the Irk under the arch opposite Muckman's Pub in Dantzic Street, and we went to school. By dinner-time I'd arrived home with a miserable face. My Father immediately asked,

"What is the matter?"
"It's my tooth," I said. "It's bad."
"Is it loose?"
"Yes," I replied.
"How long has it been loose?"
"A few days," I said; knowing what was coming next and dreading it.
"Get the strong thread out of the drawer," he said.
"What colour?" I asked, knowing it was a silly question.
"Oh, any, its for your tooth - come over here on this chair." Dad gently leaned my head back.

"Open your mouth very wide," he said, at the same time wrapping the thread around the offending tooth. "Now hold the arms of the chair tight."

This I did, putting all my strength into it. "One, two -" he pulled it out at "two", knowing I would be expecting it at "three", but by that time it was dangling in the air at the end of the cotton. Sadly, I was too old to put the tooth under my pillow for the fairies who always left you a halfpenny in its place.

I had come through Number 28 St. Michael's Square to enter the house. It used to be a great joy to me as I would be going down Red Bank, leaving Annie at the corner of Scotland trying to guess who, if anyone, had arrived home. I knew a lot of them by their first names, like Esther, Little Ada and others by my parents' conversations. Some days, if it had been wet, the house would be full when I arrived home. I would feel very important as each one would say "Hello Mary". In fact they were so friendly to me that I used to hang back and sit on a form to talk to them, but as soon as Dad appeared, I would automatically get up and go into our own house with Bulla or Fanny.

If the tea wasn't ready, I'd put a record on the old horn gramophone, or have talk with Dad's birds in their cages. Of course they never answered, except for an occasional tweet-tweet, although Gaby, the beautiful canary, sang her head off most of the time. But most of the time I would play outside with the other children. Games like cherry hog or buttons or swinging on the lamp post. Unless it was raining we were always outside. For some reason, we never got tired. Quite the opposite - you just couldn't keep us still. We were children blessed with something money couldn't buy, happiness.

CHAPTER 10

Uncut Diamonds

I was never formally introduced to any of Aunt Betsy Carter's lodgers in the normal way. "Little Ada" with her tawny coloured face and black hair parted down the middle, spoke to me for the first time when she said after taking the penny clay pipe from her mouth:

"So you are Mary, we've heard all about you", and she nodded three times. I was a bit worried about this at first, wondering what Dad had said - I hoped nothing about my past. I smiled back.

There were only four people in on this particular day, including "Little Ada". There was "Scotch Ether" who was the most beautiful crocheter I've ever met. She made the most marvellous hug-me-tights, which we now call waistcoats, in the loveliest of colours. Mother was very fond of them and had several made. Esther's husband was a collier. He was sandy, with almost white eyelashes and eyebrows; he was so pale that he reminded me of a guinea pig from Shudehill. Esther was stout and dark-haired with two dimples in her cheek when she smiled. As with most women she wore sleeper earrings.

The next one to smile at me was a "Funkum Billy", so named because he sold lavender. He would go to buy a large bag of lavender, either a pound, or two pounds or half a pound, according to the amount of money he had on him. He also bought loads of little envelopes, about half the size of a wage packet. In each envelope he put one teaspoon of the lavender seeds, and each packet cost one penny. Saturday afternoons you would find him standing in Smithfield Market, where he knew the women would be shopping.

In the evening, he would go to Belle Vue to meet the girls going to the dance halls. He rarely came back with any packets, which meant that as far as money was concerned, he'd had a good day, but it also meant of course that he might have been about all day in bitter weather.

He would come in and immediately look for my Dad to settle up for his next week's lodgings in case he "Blew it all in". He would give my Father 2/6d for the week, the price being fourpence a night (8d for a double bed), then Dad would give him twopence change. Billy would then give my Dad some money to mind for him in case again he was tempted to spend it - if a bad week came along, he would be glad of the money for food and lavender. He was always recognisable by his spectacles which were so thick, they looked like double-glazing.

Billy was a very happy little fellow, very quiet, but a hell of a nuisance when he was drunk. When he came in on Saturday night, he would do his act which was in two parts. First, a dramatic act, then a song.

He would come in with bloodshot eyes like red velvet, smiling all over his face and half way down his back. He would look at whoever was there and say, "Ladies and Gentlemen, you are going to see the greatest performance of your life - Bransby Williams in 'The Cripple from Christchurch.'" He would then put his Funkum tray around his neck, undo his laces, and take off his shoes. he would kneel down, sitting on his heels, then put a shoe on the end of each knee, like a cripple, begging. He would have his own Woodbines and matches on the tray, cap in hand saying "Help a poor beggar sir, help a poor beggar".

My parents roared with laughter, mainly, like I did, at his eyes. They looked like two spirit levels at different angles with the bubble not knowing where to go.

My Father put two-pence in his cap, my Mother a penny out of her apron pocket. They both thought it was dirt cheap. "Get up you old fool," said Old Henry, Little Ada's husband. My parents were surprised at this remark, but even more surprised when they realised that Ernie and Esther were looking rather tense. As my parents found out later, there was a reason for this. The second part was going to be played any minute. Billy would get up slowly, slip his feet into his shoes, put his cap on his chair with his tray, and totter. After lighting a cigarette from his penny-for-five packet, he placed himself very harmlessly and still smiling in front of Ernie and Esther. Ernie to me still resembled a harmless blond guinea pig, although I remember thinking that it would probably not take much to make him turn around and bite. Billy looked round at everyone and said, "You're now going to hear the Great Caruso," and then he began the song -

> "Don't go down in the mine Dad
> Dreams very often come true.
> Daddy you know it would break my heart,
> If anything happened to you.
> Go and tell my dreams to you mates,
> It's as true as the stars that shine,
> Something is going to happen today
> Dear Daddy, don't go down the mine."

Mother and Father and I clapped, just, I think, to kill the tension.

"Like it?" said Billy.

"We've heard it so often, why don't you let poor Old Caruso or whoever he is rest?" said my Dad.

"How about you then Esther," said Billy, "I think its a bloody lovely song."

Esther didn't answer.

"All right," said my Mother to help Father out, "It was very good." Mother had really put water on hot clinkers somewhat.

Billy kept right on talking. "How about you Ernie, that was for you, you're a miner, aren't you?"

"Look," said Ernie, "if you don't keep you bloody trap shut and yer tongue between your teeth, I'll shut it for yer. I've warned yer before. Who the hell wants to listen to that? Every bloody time we go down in that cage, we're wondering whether we're going to come up again." Turning to my Dad, he said "You know, Jim, only for frightening old Mrs Carter, I'd have shut him up before now." "Sorry, sorry, no offence intended," said Billy, and off he went to bed.

Little Ada and Jim were also great turns, or at least, Jim was. He was a very strong Irishman. He could have a drink and cause no trouble at all. He had been a very handsome chap in his young days. He was grey with a thick, not too long beard. Ada or Adelaine which was her real name, was like a doll, but she seemed bigger because of her many bulky skirts which she wore to keep her warm as she walked at the side of Jim whilst he sang in the streets. Ada collected the coppers and carried them in her extra large apron pockets. They were never short of a pan of ribs and cabbage, pestil or a sheep's head. They went out every single day, hail, rain or sunshine. The rain didn't trouble them in the least, because it often meant that people showed more pity especially in the pubs. Saturday was also a good day with a matinee at one theatre and a different theatre in the evening. They had quite a full life.

Jim would sing for hours outside, but he would never sing in the house unless he'd "had a couple" and he wouldn't sing at all if Billy was in.

But, all in all, they got on pretty well together. On the outside a pretty rough bunch, but deep down inside, they had a quality which now is hard to find. All they lacked was a little polish - just like uncut diamonds.

Nine years old and still an only child. I had great maternal instincts and was ever wondering if my parents would keep their promise and "get" another baby, not knowing at that age where babies came from.

In between dressing up a dolly peg with some of my clothes and feeding one of Dad's linnets one day, I decided to clean out, or to be more precise to have a root, at the bottom drawer besides the fire where all my treasures were kept; my pearl buttons, beads, buckles and odds and ends that were once Great Aunt Betsy's, and all my books and pencils. I decided to kneel down and lift the whole drawer out; as I did so, a paper slipped out and down the back of the drawer.

I put the drawer on the table and went back for the paper. Bending down to pick it up, I noticed something else. It was the box! The mystery box that had caused Mother so much excitement. Dare I look inside? No, I'd wait until my Dad was out.

I went next door, where my Mother was talking to "Jimmy the Wireworker". Jimmy was making the lengths of copper wire for his toasting forks and letter racks which he sold door to door.

"Hello, what do you want? I thought you were very quiet," said Mother.

"Where's Dad?" I asked.

"Gone to the Forum," she replied.

The Forum I think was a place somewhere in town where they had meetings.

That suited me to a tee, so I just turned and went back into our own house, bent down and lifted out the little box. I couldn't believe my eyes. It was full of golden sovereigns! There were sixty of them - I counted them. There were other coins, only small ones, but also gold. I remember thinking that Great Aunt Betsy must have been one of those people called a millionaire.

I could hear Mother's voice getting nearer, so I put the box back very quickly and also the drawer in case she guessed what I'd discovered. Sitting quietly on the green plush sofa and going over in my mind the joy of finding Aunt Betsy's treasure, I couldn't help wondering how many sovereigns she must have handled in her whole life.

There were the half sovereign earrings and three sovereign brooch of Mother's besides rings and other brooches, and Dad's two pound piece and chain in gold; the carved and engraved Waltham watch, all of which had been hers. She'd got the Midas touch it seemed.

It didn't seem right that we had all that gold yet Jimmy, or "Johnny the Tiger Hunter" or "Funkum Billy" would come in on a bad wet day bemoaning the fact that they'd all had a rotten day. The rain would have spoilt Billy's tray of lavender, and Jimmy would have dangling wet long toasting forks hanging from a wire-ring which fitted over his shoulder. Johnny sold coconut door mats. The first day he appeared for a week's lodgings, he carried a bundle of four of these mats. As no one

A Pavement artist (just like Luke) at work in Manchester in early 1900s.

was obliged to give their name, it was up to Dad to dub one for them, so Dad thought Jimmy looked as though he was on Safari, he came up with the "Tiger Hunter". On bad days, Johnny with his wet mats looked the most depressed of all. To make things a little better, the cleaner would light an extra fire in the back kitchen for them to dry their clothes.

Ada and Henry didn't mind how much it rained. Henry would sing "Poor Robert Emmett" or the "Southdown Militia" in the middle of the road outside the pubs as far away as Rochdale or Oldham and other places where they weren't known, and Ada, with her head wet and rain running down her face, would collect the money.

Apart from Ada and Henry, the others preferred the Summer. There was Luke with his flat nose. In anyone else, this would have been the sign of a violent man in my Dad's eyes, but, as he was the husband of one of our cleaners, who was a very hard-working little woman, and as he was known to be inoffensive, he passed Dad's scrutiny. They lived in a furnished room in Old Mount Street off the Meadow; every now and then he would go on the bottle, then when Alice his wife could stick it no longer, they would have a bellowing session, and she'd throw him out. He daren't come to our house drunk, so he'd stay at a men's lodging house to sober up, then he'd come and see my Dad. My Dad would tell him what a fool he was and Alice would allow him home.

Luke was nicknamed "Constable" by my Father. He was a pavement artist and drew the most fantastic chalk pictures on the flags. I remember my friend Mabel and I standing for ages watching him whilst his pictures gradually materialised - take for instance a ship on the sea with a blue sky. He started the sky with blue chalk, covering that in parts with white, touching it gently with his middle finger and working it in a circular movement making the soft clouds. The same process with two shades of green, formed the sea. His chalks he kept in a flat tin tobacco box, and by his side was a flat cap, lining upwards, for any coppers thrown in his direction.

"Doing well?" I asked, which was a silly question, as I could see for myself.

"Not bad, not bad," he answered, which meant, 'very good'.

He'd got another large piece of new untouched brown paper in his hands as if he intended drawing something on it.

"What are you going to draw on that?" I asked.

"What, this?" he asked unnecessarily.

"Yes, that" I said laughing out loud.

"It's finished," he said, also laughing - the skin drawing tight across his broken flat nose.

"Don't be daft, there's nowt on it," I said, wondering where the joke was.

"It's a brace of geese just flown out of sight," He'd won, cleverly too, my friend and I thought.

Mable was a very witty girl and as we walked away, she said "I wonder if he had white or brown sugar on his hair?"

I laughed because I knew what she meant. There were no hair lacquers in those days, so people used to make their own out of a small amount of warm water or tea with a lot of sugar in. They would dip the comb in and comb their hair to keep it tidy and in place.

"I don't know," said I, "it looked more like golden syrup."

We both laughed, and went on our way.

CHAPTER 11

Irish Paddy

Amongst our many lodgers there was an Irishman, nicknamed "Irish Paddy". One day, looking through a little hole in the paint between the letters on the window which said:-

'single beds fourpence
double bed eightpence
per night'

I saw the figure of a man. He was tall, very good-looking and strong. By the time I'd had a good look, the front door latch had clicked and in had walked Paddy. He stood in full view as he replaced the huge brass latch on the equally heavy but solid Georgian door.
"Evening Paddy." greeted my Dad. "Been a rotten day, hasn't it?"
"It has, it has, and didn't the holy angels themselves decide to swill the heavens," answered Pat. He sat down to untie the pieces of thick string that he used to keep the bottoms of his trousers out of the water in the deep holes of clay in which he worked. He started to get down the large frying pan from the shelf, and put the pan on the hob of the fireplace. Next he washed his hands in the slopstone, and to dry them, brushed his fingers through his hair. "Now forritt," he said, and into the pan he threw a large thick slice of ham; when that was part cooked, he dropped in two lovely big green-shelled duck eggs and a large piece of liver.
When they were cooked, he took them all out with a white enamelled fish slice and put them onto a medium sized meat plate, then topped and tailed three thick slices of bread in the delicious fat, and filled his large enamel pint pot. He pulled out the wooden form, threw his legs over and sat down. Then he rubbed his two hands together vigorously and pulled each finger joint, as though sitting on an organ stool about to give us a rendering of Bach's Toccata and Fugue, then he winked which meant I'm sure, "Just watch this!"
I had no reason to doubt that although Paddy had never heard of paté de fois gras, (which in any case he would have thought was a female singer) he wouldn't have swopped his meal for that. Although I had

had my tea of rabbit soup and dumplings, I felt most sure that I could help him demolish the lot if he needed help. I could actually taste the fat and feel the corner of the golden crispy fried bread crunching beneath my teeth.

Within minutes it was gone.

As I pondered where all that food had gone, I noticed that his left stockinged foot was caressing his right one, and that all his ten toes were moving happily together. His big hob-nailed boots were under my stool. "And did those feet....." I thought. Everyone liked Paddy, he was soft spoken and shy too, like Jim. I was watching his toes when he said "Isn't it hot ye are, sitting so close the the fire?"

"No, I'm just listening to the marble in the fountain, its jumping about. It needs more water in. I'll go and tell Mam." "Ah now," said Paddy "leave your Mother a'be, it's meself who will fill it."

"But you'll get sand all over your socks," I said.

"Divil of a lot of harm it will do me, sand or no sand."

Up he got, and went to the slopstone returning with two large cans full of cold water. He took off the big heavy lid from the fountain and tipped in the water. There was a fountain, or night-watchman's kettle at each side of the fire.

Paddy finally finished his tea and smoke and because he had already disturbed himself, he decided to begin his usual ritual - the preparation for going out. He pulled his thick striped Union shirt over his head, folded it, and put it on the blue and white enamelled back chair with the words "Watsons' Matchless Cleanser" on the back.

He washed and then disappeared into the back kitchen, with eyes closed, groping for the long roller towel which was hung on the back kitchen door.

Whilst he'd been having his wash, Dad had come up from the cellar with wood and coal for the morning fire. I got the dominoes ready for the nightly game which Dad and I always had after he'd finished his chores. "Evening Daddy, Evening Jim, Hello Mary," said Jimmy the wireworker on his way through to the other house. Paddy and Dad answered "Good evening." I just smiled. Paddy picked up his dirty shirt and prepared to go upstairs to change.

Noticing my Dad staring intently at his arm, he extended it towards him saying "Like it?"

"Bridie, eh?" said Dad, staring at Paddy's tattoo.

I couldn't help but wonder why I hadn't noticed it whilst he was eating his meal, but then I realised it must have been under the turn-up of his shirt sleeve. The tattoo was of a little bird with a heart between

Very typical of the houses in the Angel Meadow area. Three floors getting sunlight because of the raised 'cellars'.

its beak, an arrow from Cupid and the name "Bridie" in the centre.

Lower down the arm was a circle of roses with the name "Agnes" engraved in it.

"Very nice, new girl friend?" quipped Dad.

"I'll introduce you to her one day," said Paddy. On the other arm was just one word "Mother" inside a laurel of leaves.

"Well, what happened to Agnes then?" asked Dad.

That was something I'd been dying to ask. After a pause Paddy said, "Well you see, she was a girl I was courting in Dublin, and we intended making a go of it. But sure, hadn't me back been turned five minutes before it was she who was off with another fella. After two whole years at that!"

"Did she?" asked Dad

"Oi, she did an'all, sure, she was the divil's own," said Paddy.

"I bet that made you mad, didn't it," said Dad sympathetically.

"Sure it did, it did. Of course, I went back to Dublin to see who was the great handsome man she' got, and God Bless My Soul, he was as bald as the font he was christened in. And didn't my Mother's chickens weigh a divil more, and look a fine sight healthier than he?"

He paused "Eight stone would be all he would weigh, and she herself on the scale at thirteen."

Paddy smiled widely showing a most perfect set of teeth, the result of his regular use of soot and salt.

After a while, Paddy was changed, wearing his starched shirt done at the Prospect Laundry (I know because I handed them in at the little cellar office in Lord Street on my way to school), a smart brown suit and shoes. He took off his coat for a while to re-comb his hair, exposing his green elastic braces.

Looking very pleased with himself, he threw back his shoulders, looked with a smile at Mam and me, and said, "Its to the pub I'm going. I'm seeing Bridie in the 'Gaping Goose'. The curse of the divil himself will be upon me if I make a bugger of this courtship." He darted to the door and disappeared. After a pause, Mother said to Dad, "You know Jim, that's the first time I've ever heard Paddy swear." Mother must have thought he'd been a valet at the Vatican.

"Yes, he's a nice fellow," said Dad "but I'm surprised at him going with a girl he picked up in a pub.

"He should know what he's doing." said Mam, turning and reversing the socks and stockings which were hung on the wire line across the mantelpiece to dry.

The following Saturday, Mother sent me to Marks and Spencer's Penny Bazar for several items for the kitchen. I was just coming out when I noticed it had started to rain, so I hesitated in the doorway; as I glanced to the left I recognised the back of a strong young man dressed all in brown. It was Paddy, and with a lovely young lady. The girl noticed me first, and realising that I seemed to be very interested in them both nudged Paddy which caused him to turn around "Hello, Mary" he greeted. "This is Bridie" he said to me. "And this is little Mary" he explained to Bridie. We both just nodded and smiled to each other,

"We're just going to see your Mam and Dad; we've just got engaged," said Paddy.

"Goodie!" said I, not really knowing what to say on such an occasion. When we arrived home, Paddy introduced Bridie to my Mother. "This is my landlady," and turning to Bridie smiled, then turned back to Mother saying "This is Bridie." All this was later repeated for Dad's benefit.

Bridie was very pretty, with a gorgeous shade of copper coloured hair and hazel eyes, but I remember, I didn't like her legs. They were "growing pain" legs, a bit bandy, as though she'd had rickets. After a while, the couple went out to celebrate.

I was in bed when Paddy came in, so I didn't see him until morning

Angel Street

and it wasn't the Paddy I knew. He was pale and haggard and wasn't having any breakfast, which wasn't Paddy at all. I was worried and said "What's to do, are you ill?"

"Sure, I feel like the devil himself, hanging by his horns to a tree."

'But aren't you going to have any breakfast?" I asked.

"No, but if you'd like to go to Peter's Cellar on Dantzic Street for two Prairie Oysters, I'd be much obliged." So off I went. Two minutes later I was back with the two eggs and vinegar. In one gulp he downed the lot, shivered, went "Grr" and put back the pint pot under the tap. His colour came back almost immediately and he looked heaps better.

Later in the day, someone knocked on the door, which was unusual, as everyone knew you had only lift up the lock "See who it is," said Mother guessing it wasn't a regular. I went to the door and found Bridie standing there, smiling and showing off her ring of one small diamond as she nervously moved a little gold cross (on a gold chain round her neck) from one side to the other.

"Hello" we both chimed together, me opening the door, and Bridie walking in.

"Is Danny ready?" she asked.

"Danny?" said I, "We call him Paddy."

Mother looked as surprised as I was and even Bridie looked puzzled. Finally, Paddy came downstairs looking fit as a fiddle, the Prairie Oyster had done the trick.

"I knew you'd have a swelled head after last night" Bridie chirped" and as you were late calling for me, I decided to come here."

"Er - Paddy" I said. "Why do we call you Paddy?"

"What do you mean," he asked. In the meantime, I'd noticed a "Don't be cheeky" look on my Mother's face, but I'd already asked the question and I had to explain what I really meant.

"Well, er, I mean, Bridie calls you Danny."

"Oh that," he said. "Sure, isn't every Irishman called Paddy by the English.

Your Dad himself called me Paddy when I first came and as we were strangers then, I thought 'Sure, one name's as good as another.' My name is Daniel Patrick Monohan and my family have a farm at County Kerry. I have a brother Leo, and another Dominic. I've one sister, God bless her, by the name of Celia, although she is now Sister Bernadette, she being in a convent, having taken the veil."

After a pause, Mother said "Will you taking Bridie home to meet your parents?"

Paddy replied "Well, Mother died two years ago, God rest her soul, and I missed her very much. You see, she thought I needed more care and protection on account of my wanting leave home, as I was the only one out of the three of us who didn't like farming. I hated the dung, the silo, the dipping. So, says I, I'm off to England to make money for my marriage that, as ye know, faded out, but the Holy Mother herself must have been guiding me, because didn't I meet Bridie?"

Smiling broadly, at Bridie, he opened the door, said "See you later" and out the couple went.

Soon after their engagement, they were married and got a little house down Rochdale Road in Copper Street in the next street to Zinc Street, where one of my Mother's friends lived. But still Paddy carried on navvying and Bridie still served behind the bar at the 'Swan with Two Necks.'

We missed Paddy a lot but realised that our loss was Mr and Mrs Daniel Patrick Monahan's gain.

CHAPTER 12

The 'Half Inchers' and the 'Confidence Trickster'

Apart from my Father, who had a reputation for being a very smart man, Jack and George another two of the lodgers were like mens models. They were the only two people I never ever spoke to and they never spoke one word to me.

They were beautifully, or rather impeccably dressed in tailored suits and felt "wide-awakes" which are hats with wide brims. They even wore spats over their shoes. Jack would go out with George early in the morning dressed in navy blue. George would be in brown. When they returned, Jack would be in grey and George in salt and pepper mixture, and both would be wearing caps. One day, I asked my Dad about this but he didn't know, and said maybe it was something to do with their work. I mentioned it again suggesting "Perhaps they're detectives." When I said to Dad "have you asked Jack and George why they're always dressed up?" he replied very sternly. "No, I haven't and don't intend to, and I think you'd better keep out of their way."

I never brought the subject up again, but years after I asked my Mother if she remembered those two chaps Jack and George. What was the mystery attached to them? Why did they go out dressed one way and come back dressed differently.

"Well," said Mother, "they used to travel the horse-racing circuits. They were 'Half inchers' or pinchers of wallets. They went in high-class paddocks and were pick-pockets. Then, they'd collect their case from the station or wherever it was and change their clothes in case someone had spotted them."

The mystery of Jack and George was solved.

One day I was watching May and Hannah, two sisters-in-law making their paper flowers, when there was a gentle tap on the door. "Come in," called Mother. In walked a very gentle old lady. She was the prettiest old lady I'd ever seen, if you can say that about an old lady. She seemed to be too small to call beautiful. She was very clean, as though she had been scrubbed and her hair was snow-white and was taken right back into a bun the same as Ada's. She wore only a white apron black skirts and a black honeycomb shawl.

"Could you put me up?" she asked my Mother.

"How long for?" asked Mother.

"Just depends," said the old lady.

"What does that mean?" said Mother smiling.

The old lady looked at Hannah, May and myself and then at my Mother again.

"I'll tell you some other time," she said, "But I'll pay for a week just now." She took out her purse from her apron pocket and handed my Mother two shillings and fourpence for the week. We all moved up to let her sit by the fire. We didn't provide food, but Mother always gave a cup of tea on the first visit. My Dad returned from the bicycle shop where he'd been for a pump and seeing a new face, he smiled and said "Good evening."

Later, I took her up the stairs to bed, the fishtail gas light showing the way.

"Isn't she a lovely old woman?" said Mother to Dad.

"She is. I wonder what her name is?" he replied.

Her routine was the same each day. Out each morning and back about 4 p.m. and she always had a smile for everyone.

We had three houses but only one front door so everyone came and went through that single door. This enabled Father or Mother to know exactly who was in or out.

After about a month, Mother and Dad were shocked when this dear old soul said very quietly, "I don't think I will be staying with you much longer."

"Why, what's happened?" asked Mother very softly.

"Well to be honest I won't be able to pay my way. You see my husband died and I couldn't get on with my son, so he is in my house. I'm waiting for some money some policies and other things, but at the moment I'm stuck," she said.

Her small and angelic face clouded over. "I'm going to the Solicitors tomorrow - it should be settled shortly."

"Who is your Solicitor?" said Dad,, thinking it might be the same one as Aunt Betsy's. But she didn't seem to hear and she coughed instead. Dad didn't pursue the subject, but said "Well, what do you want money for, we won't throw you out for two and four."

"But how can I live? I've been eating in the cook-shop in the market."

"Well you can live with us until you get fixed up," said Mother. "Of course you can," chipped in Dad. That was that. She was the only on who was allowed to stop in all day, but she helped Mother by washing the pots and peeling the vegetables. She even got as far as tidying and dusting our own private house. Mother was very attached to her as she'd had no Mother since a young girl. The old lady made several visits to the Solicitors but with no luck.

One day, she told my Mother that she was slipping home whilst her son was at work. She said she didn't expect anything but bills waiting for her there as her Solicitors had got our address for her private letters.

Out she went at around two o'clock returning at six with a sheath of papers in her hands. "I told you," she said, "Bills."

"Won't your son be worried about you?" said Mam.

"That's all right - see" said Dad, handing her the six pounds. "Give it me back all together."

"All right, thanks," said Mrs Blake, having mentioned this name when talking of her house and money she couldn't collect.

"She doesn't give much away," said Mother later. "She shouldn't be having all this trouble just over her husband's Will, should she?"

Dad still got complimentary tickets for the Osborne Theatre. He only had to approach Harry, the doorman and the tickets were his. Mother, Mrs Blake and myself went. This happened for another three weeks. Free theatre, fish and chips on the way home - Mrs Blake enjoyed life to the full.

One day, out of the blue, Mother said to Dad "You know Jim, I think there's something fishy about old Mrs Blake."

"What do you mean fishy?" he asked.

"Well you know, she seems too sweet to be wholesome," Mother said.

"Now if she was noisy and loud, you'd say she was common." said Dad.

"Still, I'd like to know who her Solicitors are - if she has any that it."

"Of course she has. Good heavens, you'd doubt your own Mother," said Dad.

Later that day, Mother went to Smithfield Fish Market for some haddock, leaving Mrs Blake tidying our beautiful mahogany dresser with the lovely china ornaments, whilst Dad was cleaning out his bird cages. He had four linnets, a lark and a beautiful singing canary which was in a nice wire cage on a little round table. His, or her name was Gaby.

Something was beginning to gnaw at Dad after Mother's speech. "You can leave that Mrs Blake if you want to go out to your Solicitors," he said in a very friendly way.

"It's not Bennett, is it?" said Dad conjuring up a name of his own, thinking that if she said "yes" this would be ample proof that she was a fraud. But Dad's fears were allayed when she said "No, it isn't Bennett; it's a queer foreign name. I can't say it properly, but I could write it down." This was rather unusual as most people then couldn't read. She was evidently quite educated, as far as reading was concerned.

At about one thirty, she washed her face and combed her hair and was putting her shawl around her shoulders, when my Father said very charmingly "Oh, just hang on a minute Mrs Blake, I'll walk with you, I'm going into Oldham Street."

"All right," she said "but I've got to go to Oxford Road."

"That's all right, I want to see what's on at the Palace anyway."

They both made for the door, both smiling with Mrs Blake saying "See you later" to me. Oldham Street was only five minutes away with my young legs, but it would take my Dad and Mrs Blake longer, of course.

"You've no need to go all that way to Oxford Road," she said to Father.

"That's all right, it's a lovely day," and on they walked, until they came to a very imposing building where she stopped and pushed open the door. She held open the door for my Dad to enter also and they went to a corridor upstairs.

"Is this it then?" Dad asked, as they walked up the stairs.

"Yes, sit there, I won't be long," she said, pointing to an upholstered short form seat.

Dad sat down, feeling very ashamed of his thoughts about the poor old soul. Won't Polly feel a fool, he thought. He got up to look out of the window at the people passing on top of the trams. Opposite, in a window was a clock which showed the time at 2.45 p.m. He sat down again looking at the people working in the offices opposite. After a while, he took out his watch to find it was three o'clock. He began to think that she must be making some headway.

He heard the trundle of another tram, and after the trolley on the overhead wires had passed, he looked for the second time at the offices across the way, wondering if they were also Solicitors. He was thinking to himself "What was the name of that Solicitor of Mrs Blake's?" She mentioned that she couldn't pronounce it. It was a foreign name.

My Father was getting a bit fed up with all this waiting when almost two hours after their arrival the door slowly opened. He jumped up to greet the old lady, but felt bitter disappointment when he saw a young man emerging - a young man who had walked past him earlier.

He sat down again thinking it was about time he found the Solicitor. When he heard the young man reach the street, he opened the door and found himself in a long corridor with offices at either side filled with typist who sounded as if they were working overtime. There were different names on the doors but none which sounded foreign. In fact, he couldn't even find a Solicitors office.

Eventually, he came to a lift and staircase, one for up and one for down. He didn't know which to take thinking he might miss her if he went onto another floor. He stood leaning casually on the hoist, knowing that he couldn't possibly miss her which ever direction she came from, she would have to pass him if he stopped there.

The same young man came up again from the street and looked strangely at my Father. He didn't say anything - he just went into his office. Seconds later, a man emerged and made his way towards my Father.

"Who are you waiting for mate?" he asked.

"An old lady" said my Dad.

"What, one about twenty-one," said the man sarcastically.

"No, I came with an old lady to see her Solicitors," said my Father.

"What Solicitor? There isn't any Solicitors in this building," said the man.

"But she came through that door there. I'm not meeting her, I brought her myself," said Dad beginning to feel rather uncomfortable.

"All right, what's the bloke's name," snapped the man.

"Oh him - well, I don't know. She didn't know either."

"So, she has a Solicitor and she doesn't even know his name. Listen mate, if you're not out of this building in two minutes, I'll fetch the coppers."

My Father didn't need any prompting and began to move when the young chap came back with his boss. He approached my Dad and said

"This young fellow thought you were a detective at first."

Dad wondered where all this was leading. The man continued.

"Did I hear you say you brought an old lady to see a Solicitor?"

"Yes, that's right," said Dad.

"Was she very small and pleasant?"

"Yes, she is?" smiled Dad.

"Is?" said the man.

"Yes," said Dad, puzzled, "do you know who I mean now?"

"No, I don't know her, and neither do you. I think she must have conned you if it's the same one I've heard of. Does she owe you anything?"

"Well," said Dad, "as a matter of fact she does. She lodges in my house in Angel Meadow. Her husband died and her assets have not been settled, so I helped her out."

"Assets and living in a lodging house?" said the man again sarcastically.

"Well, she reckoned she didn't belong around here. She has her own little house, but can't get on with her son," said Dad.

"You didn't fall for that one, did you?" said the Boss.

"That same old girl has pulled that trick before."
"Thanks for telling me," said Dad "I'll tell her to hand over my six quid when she comes out and then give her a wide berth. It's a good job I came with her today."
"You'll not get your six quid mate!" said Know-All.
"Why, what do you mean?" asked Dad.
"Well, she's done what she's done each time before - buggered off down those stairs into the street." (Indicating the flight of steps at the side of the hoist where my Father was standing.)

Dad felt dazed. He really couldn't believe it and when he got home my Mother couldn't believe the news either.

"Well, fancy that - a confidence trickster. You know, I was only thinking last night, we never saw those supposed bills, they could have been anything," exclaimed Mother.

"Yes, and we never even intruded by asking what the money was for, because six or seven pounds is a hell of a lot of money," said Dad.

"Six or seven?" said Mother. "What about her food and lodgings?"

They both paused, then Dad said "I suppose you live and learn in this business." After a pause Mother said "Eh, it's a good job she didn't know anything about the box."

Dad replied "Oh nobody knows anything about the box."

I had just taken out my rosary beads from inside one of the brass knobs on the bed. I'd unscrewed it really because I'd put my odd coppers in the knob on the left. Inside the knob on the right, I kept my little black beads that were once Aunt Betsy's. Seeing that they were safe and that I hadn't been robbed, I replaced the top of the knobs in time to hear.

"No, no-one knows anything about the box."

I had my back turned to them, so I smiled to myself thinking "Well at least Dad thinks no-one know about the box." My Father felt too ashamed to go to Goulden Street Police Station to report the episode of the clever old girl. He didn't even mention it to his friend P.C. Hilary Friar, a young policeman who seemed to be very fond of my Father. He called every beat and was partial to a nice cup of tea.

CHAPTER 13

My First Boyfriend

My favourite person in the house we called number three was a good looking chap of about thirty whose name was Mickie Pye. He "Played the pubs" with Joey his ventriloquist doll. Joey was not much smaller than me. He had pink cheeks, large eyes and very crispy black hair. He was fully dressed in a navy blue suit and his body was made of wood. His head, which was a solid block, was attached to a thick round stick with a wire which you worked through a hole in his back.

Mickie taught me the finer points of ventriloquism. How to keep my eyes on the move, as though I was only listening to Joey. He told me that if I kept my eyes on one spot on the floor or walls whilst I talked for Joey, I would look more of a dummy than the doll. That part needed more training than the actual job of keeping your lips still, and almost closed. Although I was a very mature and serious child in many things, I couldn't keep my face straight, when, after getting all serious, say, to begin the song "On the Blue Ridge Mountain of Virginia," I would just catch a glimpse of "Little Ada" and "Scotch Esther" and all the others who would come into the room to see the "show." I would just burst out laughing. Mick would say "Come on, let's be serious." I would then sing a song, do a bit of conversation patter,and tell the now very old joke where the two Irishmen decided to go back to Ireland in a rowing boat, but decided half-way across to return to England as they had got very tired, intending to do the other half tomorrow. I remember I'd asked Joey if he had a girl friend yet and he would say he was waiting for a letter from a young lady he had proposed to. I'd say "Oh, I forgot. I've just picked this up the lobby; it's for you, but I don't believe its from a young lady."

Joey would say "all right, open it and read it to all these people." The envelope would be unsealed and so it was easy to take out the letter. I would begin;

My dearest Adoration.

In due consideration of the greatest reputation I have an inclination to become your relation. I will move my habitation to a near situation for the course of conversation with you my adoration.

If this my supplication meets with your appreciation, then meet me

at the station, and we'll be married on speculation
Yours in anticipation,
Sensation."

Mickie was always trying to persuade my Dad to let me pursue a career on the stage but Dad would repeat "The only stage Mary will get on will be on the landing stage carrying a parcel." This was a reference to porters carrying luggage at ports like Liverpool.

Mickie later bought himself a large doll as big as himself - I can't make out now whether he was a Scout Master or an Australian. I remember he had a large brimmed hat, khaki shirt and shorts and was called Horace. He was the latest thing in new inventions. He would actually smoke in between the patter! He had a tube with a rubber bulb attached to the opening of his back where his long wooden neck was. Mick would put the cigarette from a penny Woodbine packet in Horace's mouth, strike a match and pretend to light the cigarette at the same time squeezing, then relaxing the bulb every so often with his other hand. Hey Presto! He smoked better than Mickie - mind you- because Mickie was a non-smoker.

I never liked Horace. He wasn't at all lovable like Joey.

I was only about nine years old when one day Mickie put Joey on my knee. As usual, I just looked up and smiled then looked at Joey with great affection.

"Do you like him?" asked Mick.

"Oo - yes, I love him!" I said.

"Right," said Mick. "He's your first boyfriend." I didn't even know if I was supposed to give an answer. My Mother did, though, as she said "What do you mean?"

"I mean I've given it to her," he said.

When the penny dropped, I never even answered then. I was too excited, so excited that I just squeezed Joey like I would a child. Maybe it was because I was still the only child at nine and I desperately needed a child to hold. After this moment of emotion, I noticed that the house was very quiet. When I looked up, everyone who was in was in tears - including Mickie Pye. My Mother finally spoke.

"You know you shouldn't say that Mickie. What will you do for a living?"

"I've got another," he said. He went upstairs and brought down Horace.

"Jim will give you something for Joey." Mother said.

"Did I ask for anything?"

"Well no - but...." began Mother.

"Well, we'll forget it" Mickie added.

The height of entertainment for many children — listening to the barrel organ.

Needless to say that was the start of many happy hours with my friends on the front step singing "The Blue Ridge Mountains of Virginia."

To me, Lizzie seemed a funny woman. She had a thick moustache which used to frighten me. Her eyebrows were black, they went straight across her forehead and met like a thick piece of velvet ribbon. She was the only one who always wore a large hat with a big brim. Her belly was big, and she never fastened the bottom buttom of her coat.

Although she was clean, like everyone else, she went either to Osbourne Street or Red Bank Baths once a week for 2d, she never seemed to do her hair properly. Instead of putting it in a bun, or a plait brought over from each side and fastened on the top like my Mother, Lizzie wore her hair wrapped around brown hair pads, which always showed through her grey hair.

Tom was very sarcastic with Lizzie, although at the same time Mother thought Lizzie very marred. The least thing seemed to make her cry. Unknown to Lizzie Dad had a name for her - "The Scotch Mist" on account of her tears.

Tom wasn't really bad at all. I used to be fascinated by his wax moustache. He would sit for ages twiddling it around and around his fingers until he got it as stiff as two fire irons: I remember Mother saying that if he caught it with his cigarette, he'd burn to death because he'd that much wax on it.

That left just one remaining lodger and one that I loved dearly. Her name was Mary Ann Moohan. Poor Mary Ann. She worked like a slave. She would leave the house at eight o'clock in the morning to go to work in several houses in Cheetham Hightown. She would clean and scrub some days, and do family washes other days. She'd light the boiler fires with coal and wood in wet draughty cellars and it would be six o'clock when she got home. She always wore clogs with a strap. She would tell us she would get half a crown for scrubbing, boiling, mangling, rinsing and starching clothes and bedding for a large family. In fact she used to swear that two families wash would be put in for the price of one. If she was lucky she reckoned she would also get a couple of sandwiches if she hadn't taken her own food.

She loved to get in from work, brew a pint of tea, sit on the steel stool at the side of the fire, cut up her thick twist, rub it between her palms and then put it in her clay pipe and smoke it, after closing the little tin lid door which covered the top. She was a widow, very similar to Little Ada, with a lovely bronze weather-beaten skin and hair tied straight back in a bun. She'd wear several dark skirts and a large double pocket apron and grey woollen shawl about her shoulders. Like Ada too, she was as straight as a model.

A lot of these lodging house women walked very straight, I'm sure it was because they didn't have soft easy chairs to slouch in.

Whenever she saw me Mary Ann would ask what I had learned at school and perhaps also ask me what was on at the Cosy Corner, all the while puffing away at her clay pipe. She always went to bed early that was unless she went with me to the pictures. I had to do with Ada what other children had to do for the illiterates at the pictures, that was to read the sub-titles to them as they'd never learnt to read themselves.

How we loved such thrills on the screen as "The Million Dollar Mystery," "The Black Hand Gang," and "The Perils of Pauline" with Pearl White. Then there were the funny people like Ben Turpin with his two left eyes. We used to go to the Little Cinema Picture House in Dalton Street, on Rochdale Road. The cinema was situated by the Long Entry where the young lads would go to the lavatory behind a curtained door, lift up the emergency bar and let their pals in who didn't have enough money for a ticket. It was Mary Ann's great pleasure in life and she got as much of a laugh as we children did.

So those were the occupants of our three houses on Angel Meadow, the lodgers, my Dad, my Mam and me, still only a child. Nine years old and what seemed a life-time behind me. But as I later found out there was much, much more to come....

CHAPTER 14

Bandbox Lettie

One day Mam and I were busy trying to fill the very large salt box used when anyone was cooking.

We had been nearly an hour chopping off blocks from a large salt brick and rolling each lump out with the wooden rolling pin, until it was like powder. We were just wrapping up the remainder in an old Sunday Umpire when there was a gentle knock on the door.

"Come in," called Mother.

We heard the door open and close gently, and in walked a young woman. She was wearing an old grey coat which dropped around her ankles, on her head she had a black silk scarf and on her feet once expensive grey suede boots fastened at the side with pearl buttons. In her hand she carried a bandbox. I was absorbing the details of her dress when I heard a gentle voice.

"Could you please find me a bed for the night?".

"Are you ill, you look very pale?" Mother replied.

"I have been, but I'm alright now," said the girl, "I've just come out of hospital."

"Sit yourself down, I'll make you a drink," Mother said re-assuringly. This was unusual, normally my parents didn't provide food for the lodgers. Obviously Mother regarded her as an exception.

The girl sat by the side of the fire and was about to begin her meal when my Father returned from cleaning the windows in Angel Meadow.

"Good evening," said Dad sternly.

"Good evening," the girl replied rather hesitantly.

"Its alright," interrupted Mother, "finish your meal.".

Dad began to walk into our private house and was closely followed by Mum.

"You know Jim, that poor thing's only come out of hospital this morning."

"How do you know?" answered Dad, "How do you know she isn't a prostitute; how long does she think she's stopping?"

"Only one night - Good God," interrupted Mother, storming back into the lodging house.

The girl had developed a nice rosy glow on her face. Mother sat next to her and I sat on the steel stool by the side of the fire.

"Have you no home of your own love?" Mother asked, "No family?"

"I might as well have none," the girl answered, "they just don't want to know me, see... I've... well... just had a baby but it died. Dad couldn't face his friends and I couldn't face the cold looks any more."

"Well you better get some sleep. Mary take her to number one" Mother ordered.

"But number one's a double room," I began.

"I know, I know," said Mum, "take her to number one."

Next morning the girl was up and out before anyone else got down for breakfast.

"Mam, that girl in number one's gone out already...." I began.

"Number one - what girl?" demanded Dad.

"Well," said Mum, "there was no-one else in number one last night."

"She sleeps in the long room with Mary Ann and all the others," said Dad, "otherwise she's out."

"But Jim, she's not like the others," pleaded Mum, "she's sort of refined."

"Refined! Refined! Oh Polly," sighed Dad and sat down.

Later that day we were sitting having tea in our own house when we heard the lodging house door open. We could usually tell who had come in by the greeting but on this occasion there was a long silence. You could tell that we were all thinking the same thing as we all got up and started making our way through the connecting door. Sitting by the side of the fire was the frail-looking girl, bandbox tied to her wrist.

"Put her in the long room," Dad whispered, "we're not having single girls sleeping in double rooms."

As Mother approached the girl, whose eyes were peering out through a careless streak of blond hair on her forehead, I saw in front of my eyes the lady in the "Sign of the Cross" picture and the words, "Is it her faith which makes her so beautiful, or does she beautify her faith?" and I began to wonder if perhaps she had been a nun, and if she had, why had God let her baby die?

"Where've you been all day love?" Mother asked.

"Cleaning," replied the girl. "In hospital a lady gave me an idea where to go to get a job cleaning for the Jews and I went early so as to light their fires."

This seemed to give the girl some sort of respectability and she was allowed to stay, and eventually she was given her own key. As the days went by I came to like the girl more and more. I discovered her name was Lettina but I called her Lettie, and we played dominoes almost every night. Even my Dad began to show genuine concern for her.

She'd been with us for nearly three months when we began our preparations for Christmas. The house was draped with bunting and a piece of mistletoe was hung over the bar of each gas jet. All the shops were decorated with Christmas Fayre and even the garden seemed lovely. I was thinking that this must be the happiest time of my life when one morning I realised that Lettie hadn't left for work. I dashed upstairs and knocked on the door. There was no answer.

"Lettie," I called, "Aren't you going to work?"

Still there was no reply. I was frightened and fled downstairs to my Mother.

"Maam, Maam," I gasped, Lettie's locked in and won't answer."

"Oh my God," gasped Mother, "Jim, Jim quickly; fetch the spare key for number one - Lettie's locked in and doesn't answer - she must be ill."

My father tried the key but the other key was still in the opposite side of the lock and he couldn't open the door. Fortunately the double bedrooms were like cubicles and open at the top so father climbed over and undid the door from the inside. Mother rushed in, "Jim. she looks ill to me, you'll have to get your bike and fetch the doctor."

The doctor arrived almost on the wheels of my Dad's bike and had soon made the diagnosis.

"Your daughter's got pneumonia and she'll have to come out of the draughty room."

"She's not our daughter," Mother replied, "she only lodges here."

"Well she'll have to go to the hospital," said the doctor.

"You mean the workhouse!" Mother asked.

"Call it what you will."

She was taken away to hospital leaving us all very dejected.

"They asked me her name and I couldn't tell them, apart from 'Lettie,' said mother.

"I wonder if her name is in her bandbox." After some discussion the hat box was brought down from under the bed and placed in the centre of the table.

The first thing to catch our eye was a black velvet evening purse covered in small black glass beads. It contained one shilling, two halfpennies and one half-crown. There were also two pawn tickets; one for a slave bangle pledge for ten shillings at Harry Crowe's and the other for a pair of brown shoes pawned at Piggy Riley's for four shillings, and at the bottom of the box an envelope. Mother picked it up and and examined it.

"Look at this," she exclaimed.

It was a picture of a lovely young blond woman with large blue sparkling eyes. It was Lettie and next to the photograph, a birthday card sent by Charles to Lettie at an impressive address in Cheshire.

"I knew she was well bred," said Mother with satisfaction, handing the card to Dad.

"So that's where she belongs," Dad exploded, "so-called well bred parents and their child lying at death's door in some hospital. I couldn't do that to a dog, what her father's done to her."

After further discussion, Mother decided to write to the address on the envelope. They agreed not to mention Angel Meadow and wrote:

"Your daughter Lettie is in Crumpsall Hospital and it may be wise to visit as soon as possible."

My father visited the hospital but was so upset at seeing her he vowed never to go again.

"She won't live. I'm sure she won't live," he kept repeating.

It was up to Mother now to do the visiting. As she was sitting by the side of the bed, the voice of a frail old lady from the next bed whispered.

"Your girl's a bit better today Missus."

"I'm glad," replied Mother, "but she's not my daughter, she belongs to a friend."

"Oh," said the woman, pausing for a second.

"I thought you and that man who came a few nights back were her parents." There followed a longer pause..." She had some grand visitors today, a fine pair in fancy clothes, you know, big hat and what not.

She tried to impress Mother by moving her thin, bony arms around her head in the shape of a hat.

"Was that her folk?" said the woman.

"Probably, probably," replied Mother.

On her next visit, Mother had to wait outside the ward, the sister had told her Lettie had already got visitors and only two were allowed for each patient. She peered round the door and after seeing Lettie chatting happily to her parents, left the hospital and began to walk home. We were all so relieved, it was almost Christmas Eve and Lettie was getting visits from her parents. Lettie continued her recovery and had more visits from them. Mother would wait on the driveway leading to the hospital, until the grand couple had finished their visiting then pop in for a chat. The story of the bandbox, the envelope and the letter to Cheshire gradually emerged.

"Oh how can I ever repay you," said Lettie.

"Well," replied Mother, "there's a saying which begins, 'I shall pass this way but once.....'"

The hospital eventually allowed Lettie to go home and we began to clear out her old clothes and boots, but not before I carefully cut off the ten grey pearl buttons. I unscrewed the top half of the brass bed knob on the bed and gently placed the buttons inside before screwing the knob tightly back. We saw nothing more of Lettie until almost twelve months later.

I'd been busy making paper for the toilets from handkerchief sized pieces of old newspaper, like the John Bull and the Sunday Umpire, tied at the corner with a piece of string.

I was tidying the table which was strewn with all sorts of interesting cuttings I'd been reading when I saw through the little clear spot on the painted windows, a taxi pulling up at the door. We all thought there had been a mistake, for out stepped a very lovely young lady. She had her back to me as she talked to the driver but I'll never forget my reaction as she began to turn.

"Mam, Mam," I cried, "here's Lettie."

"Oh, Lettie, Lettie, come in," said Mother.

I sat by the window and Lettie and my mother sat in front of me with their backs to me. I was transfixed with her beautiful purple hat which was trimmed with birds' feathers. As she moved her head the greens and the reds in the feathers seemed to change colours. Two very large hat pins with rainbow coloured pearl tops held the hat in place in her lovely, thick, golden blond hair.

I walked round in front of them. Beneath the grey wool cloth coat was a lovely purple dress trimmed with dozens of the tiniest glass beads you've ever seen. There were grey pearl buttons down her coat, and to my amazement and delight, she was wearing grey suede boots identical to the ones she was wearing when she first arrived at our house, but of course, these were complete with all the buttons and had black patent leather toes, back and heels. I remember thinking she must love grey.

Mam and Dad took her into our house and brought out the best china for tea. All too soon Lettie was getting ready to go home. She looked at me and put her arm round my shoulder.

"Where might I have been if it hadn't been for you?" she asked.

I rushed out of the room and up to the bedroom where I unscrewed the top part of the bed knob and took out the ten pearl buttons. By the time I had got down-stairs, Mother and Father and Lettie were standing at the door.

"Lettie," I said slowly, "I like your hat and boots, they are just like the ones you wore when you lived here only you were two buttons short on the others."

Lettie looked amazed. I went on, holding out my handful of buttons.

"I took these off your old boots before my mother threw them out. Would you like them in case you should lose any off yours?"

"Yes, I would, thank you," said Lettie as she stepped into the taxi. Her gorgeous blue eyes filled with tears.

CHAPTER 15

Christmas 1913

The Christmas of 1913 was to be the happiest of my life. I had my parents, the thirty-two regulars in our other house and some extra occasional visitors, and a collection of free gifts like barley sugar sticks and pieces of cake from the local shops. But the one present I really wanted was still eluding me. People would always ask you what you were having for Christmas. In my case I always answered, "I want my mother to get a baby."

I must have been very naive not to realise that the lump around my mother's middle was anything but shortage of whalebone in her stays.

We had been out on Christmas Eve to Smithfield Market to buy a wreath for Aunt Betsy's grave. The 'pot man' was busy trying to persuade you to believe your Christmas dinner would taste nicer on the row of plates he had lined up on his arm, and the 'boiled sweets man' was tempting you with a large humbug he had just made before your eyes. We bought apples for the apple sauce, onions for the stuffing and some nuts and Shrewsbury biscuits for Dad from the biscuit shop on Swan Street. These, and a canary which we bought from the pet shop in Tib Street as a companion to our other bird, Gaby, were to be his Christmas presents. When we arrived home some young carol singers were at the door singing.

"Christmas is a coming, the goose is getting fat,
Please put a penny in the old man's hat,
If you haven't got a penny, a farthing will do,
If you haven't got a farthing - God Bless You."

How could you confess to not having a farthing? I took a penny out of the brass knob on the top of the bed and gave it to them.

I had two mince pies and Dad suggested I go to bed. I didn't mind, the sooner I went to bed the sooner Father Christmas would come. Mother gave me a black woollen stocking and I hung it on the bed knob. As I began to get ready for bed there was a disturbance underneath our window. A fight was in progress and soon two bobbies arrived to sort the men out. I couldn't make everyone out but I was sure Esther was in the crowd. Eventually the men were taken away in a Black Maria and everyone dispersed. I got into bed, put my feet on the warm oven plate and was soon asleep.

I was up at eight o'clock on Christmas morning examining the contents of the stocking. I found a lovely muff from my mother, a diablo from my father and other presents from Grandad, Aunt Theresa and my other relations.

I joined the rest of the family downstairs, still wearing my red flannel nightie with my hands tucked firm in my new muff.

We all wished each other Happy Christmas.

"Happy Christmas - huh?" snorted Esther.

"What's the matter Esther?" said Henry innocently.

"Well," said Esther, "Ernie and Funkum Billy had the darbies clapped on them last night and they are in Gould Street Police Station."

So that was the disturbance last night, I thought, Ernie and Billy fighting and Esther refereeing. It seems that Ernie object to singing to Esther and, as they had all had their fill a fight ensued. Dad went straight away to bail them both out.

As money was short, most of the lodgers went out to work, at least for a few hours. We went to see Grandad and Uncle John Henry in Fennel Street. Grandad was enjoying his favourite drink of hot beer. He would put a poker in the fire until it was red hot and then put it in the beer. It would make a loud 'shnuffle, schnuffle' noise, then he would drink it. He reckoned what with the beer, the iron from the poker and charcoal from the fire, it was the finest thing for the stomach.

When we got home, Aunt Lucy and Uncle Tommy along with Aunt Maggie, my mother's sister from London, had come for tea. I liked Aunt Lucy and I decided to call Dad's new canary after her. It was only years later that I realised Lucy was in fact a male.

The Christmas celebrations were soon over and January, with its rain and cold, came around. Mother was not well and was having a lie down on the bed when two new lodgers arrived enquiring about a room. I didn't want to get Mother out of bed, so after checking to see if it was alright, took their eightpence and gave them room number three. The man seemed very nice and the woman had fair hair plaited at either side of her head and tied at the tope with a hairpin. But there was something else about her which was unusual; her ears were split at the end of the lobes and she had tatoos on her arms. I went to tell Mother.

"Good God," she cried, "that's Tiger Lily - her earrings have been dragged out while she's been fighting, whatever will your Dad say?"

Mother jumped out of bed and peered through the downstairs door. "It's her alright, thank goodness they've only booked in for one night.

They must have realised your father was out and I was not around."

My father came home and although he was obviously infuriated, he said nothing to me. I went to bed.

Around two o'clock I heard a terrible commotion. A man was shouting and, it seemed, crying in pain. I thought at first that it might be my father and, worried that he might get a knock on his legs I rushed downstairs.

Mother and Father were standing looking at Tiger-Lily who had the man by his hair and was dragging him around, he was wearing nothing but his combinations.

"She was robbing me," he cried, "she was robbing me."

Mother saw me standing in the doorway and as the couple were escorted out by two burly policemen she took me back to bed.

"Was she a robber, Mam?" I asked, "her husband kept saying that she'd robbed him."

"Oh no," replied Mother after thinking for a while., "he hadn't given her any wages so she thought she'd take some out of his pocket." Once again my naivety showed as I accepted her explanation. Even had she told me the truth I wouldn't have understood the meaning of the term prostitute.

All this time Mother kept putting on weight; now her skirt and apron strings would hardly meet around her waist and I was no wiser. Until one day I couldn't find my nightie. I asked Mam where it was and she told me to look in the chest of drawers upstairs. Naturally, I opened the top drawer first. My nightie wasn't there, at least not on the top, but there were other things which made my heart jump with joy. There were napkins and nighties and lots of other baby things. I was so happy I nearly cried.

"Mam, Mam, who are those napkins and things in the top drawer for?"

"For the baby," she answered, "our baby, its coming in a few days."

I was so excited I couldn't sleep. I told all my best friends first then everyone else in the house. Everyone expressed great delight and surprise; little did I know that far from being the first to hear the news, I was probably the last.

I went to church each day to ask God to make sure he wrapped it up and looked after it on the way from Heaven, so that, unlike our other baby, it wouldn't die, and then on the third day my hopes were realised and the baby arrived and it was a girl.

I wanted to dash straight in to see Mother and my baby sister but Auntie Lizzie stopped me.

"Don't make a noise, your mother feels ill and the baby is very delicate, we're not sure whether we will rear it as its heart isn't very strong."

I felt very downhearted and kept thinking that all this was happening because I wasn't going to church on a Sunday.

I couldn't wait any longer and crept into the bedroom. My Mother explained that the baby wasn't very strong and that she couldn't be put in water and had to be gently covered in olive oil for a few months. I looked at the baby at my Mother's side. She was the colour of a plum, a sort of reddish-blue, and her teeny-weeny face was peeping out from her mummy-like wrapping, but I didn't mind that at all. She was our baby, our very own.

I was in a dream and just couldn't leave the baby alone. I kept thinking that we may not have her for long so I was determined to sit near her all the time and to pray each night to St. Anthony.

I felt as if I had to tell as many people as possible, Ada and Henry and Mary Anne asked what we were going to call the baby.

"Evelyn," I answered, "Mum says she likes Evelyn."

Esther said she would crochet something nice for her and Mick and Priscilla and Bill all suggested that now I'd have to take a back seat. When I was sure everyone knew about the baby I decided to make my way to bed. Dad had filled the old herb bottle with sand and warmed it up in the oven and as I warmed my feet I prayed to St. Anthony.

> "The Sea obeys and fetters break.
> And lifeless limbs thou doest restore
> Whilst treasures lost are found again,
> Young and old thine aid implore
>   Amen."

I said this prayer each night along with The Lord's Prayer and two Hail Marys and each day our tiny baby got a little bit stronger.

CHAPTER 16

Mary Anne

Mother was having quite a bad time with the baby which had to be fed often with only short intervals between each feed. There was special washing, boiling, starching and ironing and, to make matters worse, Dad's bad legs were playing him up.

It was Friday and Mother had asked me to do Saturday's shopping, Mary Anne, one of the lodgers, offered to take me.

I was extremely fond of Mary Anne and I was rather pleased at the prospect of going shopping with her, especially since I'd longed for some time to discover how she came to have a good supply of fruit in her room.

Mary Anne soon realised that I was paying more attention to the fruit on the chiffonier than on the conversation and asked me if I wanted an apple or orange. I was a little disappointed because I preferred pears but she hadn't mentioned them so politely I took an apple - minus one slice.

"Mary Anne", I questioned, "where's the other slice?" pointing to the missing part which had now gone quite brown.

"Oh, I cut that off because it was a little bruised."

"But they've all a bit missing," I added.

"They were all a bit bruised," she replied, "any more questions?"

I accepted her explanation and finished eating my apple putting the core in the box where she kept her bits of rubbish.

"Would you like a pear?" Mary Anne added.

I picked up a large, juicy pear and, still somewhat puzzled, went back downstairs.

I couldn't get this incident out of my mind as we set off early on Saturday morning for the shops

The market stall holders started work at 4 o'clock, so when Mary Anne and I arrived at ten everything was in full swing. The fruit and vegetable men were selling their wares and Joe, the weighing machine man, who was Great Grandad's neighbour, was busy cleaning his chair with a handbrush.

As we turned into Swan Street on our way to Oldham Street, Mary Anne gave me a tug on the shoulder.

"Here you are, round here first," she whispered.

I followed her down a side street which led to the fruit and vegetable part of Smithfield Market. Her eyes began to dart all over the ground.

"What are you doing, Mary Anne?" I asked.

"I'm looking for the best fruit," she replied.

I couldn't understand what she was talking about, the best fruit on the floor! But Mary Anne seemed to know what she was doing so I followed her round the corner.

Suddenly the place was full of people, men women and children all bending towards the ground. Several of them acknowledged Mary Anne's presence as she joined them sorting through all the rubbish. At regular intervals a hand would emerge clasping a bruised apple or orange or pear, discarded by the stall keepers because of the slight discolouration.

"Make sure the apples are hard," Mary Anne advised as I joined the crowd.

Altogether we collected about three pounds of assorted fruit and placed them carefully in Mary Anne's black apron before continuing with the shopping.

"Where have you been?" said Mother when we arrived home.

"Picking fruit," I replied "on the market."

"On the market floor you mean."

The wholesale market, corner of Swan Street & Rochdale Road, an ideal place for picking up fruit.

The new baby showed progress slowly gaining in weight and although she was still in what the doctor called 'the vital period', the first three months of her life, the time had come for me to take her out for her first walk.

I'd waited years for this occasion and I was thrilled to bits when, arriving home from the market, I was met by my Mother who had already prepared the bassinette and tucked Evelyn in.

"Don't keep her out long," shouted Mother as I skipped off down the street, "she'll need changing."

I took the baby past Kings the chip shop, down to the corner, round into Dantzic Street and up Miller's Lane till I got to Baxdendales where they sold the poshest bathroom suites. The only bath with hot running water that I'd ever seen was at the Corporation Baths near Piggy Riley's and I stood and stared in Baxendales window wondering whoever bought such luxury. Then I glanced at Evelyn and though "Well, I got something better than a marble bathroom." I crossed over Miller's Lane to look into the windows of Hildersheimers where they sold the most fantastic oil paintings in gold leaf frames. My favourite was 'Last Watch of the Hero' with those sad, wet eyes which always seemed to fill me with an uncanny presence.

I crossed over the road again and set off up Rochdale Road past the Little George beerhouse and Danny Milligan's donkey and cart which was parked outside while Danny had a pint.

After I'd passed the pub I stopped at the cloggers to have my clogs ironed; I was very heavy on irons because I was always 'sparking', so it seemed an ideal opportunity to have them done.

When they were finished, it was time for me to head for home, past the cookshop with its huge rabbit and meat and potato pies, the Weaver's Arms beerhouse and eventually back to Angel Meadow. I felt as proud as punch.

We were now midway through 1914. Many of the lodgers had changed but the old faithfulls were still with us. Mary Anne, Lizzie and her husband, Ada and Henry, loveable Bill, Mick, Sam and Kitty. Of all of them, Kitty was the odd one out.

She dyed her hair with Titian henna which made it a bright shade of red. My friend Veronica said it looked like she was on fire, and other people suggested she looked more like a Rhode Island Red. But no matter how happy they all were you could tell something was worrying them.

Funkum Billy could only just manage to raise his funny smile and Mick, with his suntan and gold tooth, didn't seem his usual self. Everyone seemed to be talking about the war; I'd even heard my Dad talking about

Angel Street, in Angel Meadow, watching the world go by.

the 'bad' news to Mother. Ada and Henry were more concerned than anyone though. They had two sons, Michael and Joseph, at St. Joseph's Industrial School, and sure enough, when the war started in August, Michael, the older of the two. was drafted into the army.

It seemed funny that, in the middle of all the commotion surrounding the outbreak of war, I should be having my birthday. But on the 31st August 1914, I reached the grand age of ten. I received lots of money from everyone and when I counted it I'd totalled nine and sixpence. I told Dad the news and he added another sixpence to make it ten bob and I had my first real savings.

The outbreak of war meant all sorts of new regulations, one of them being that all lodging house keepers had to register everyone who was in their house. I had to go to Four Yards near King Street to a shop called Meredith, Ray and Littler to buy one hundred registration forms for the lodgers to fill in. They nearly all said they couldn't write so they put an X instead and those who could write put either Smith or Jones. I did my little bit for the war effort by filling in our name and address alongside that of the lodgers, it really made me feel important.

Michael, Ada and Henry's son, was now in his full uniform having joined the Territorial Army. When he came in for the last time before leaving Manchester, Mother put on the gramophone and we all sang, "Jolly good luck to the girl who loves a soldier."

He looked so handsome in his khaki.

This was for some time the only reminder to me that there was a war. Things went on very much the same as always. I was still taking Evelyn for her walks in the pram to Smithfield Market, she was old enough now to be able to sit up and watch the pigeons, rabbits and cocks, and hens and chicks in their cages. I would leave her watching the furry creatures and browse through the hundreds of old books on the old bookstall lit by tilley oil lamps.

One particular day we'd been to see the canaries and linnets in the shop on Tib Street and were just passing the pet shop with its kittens and puppies when Evelyn suddenly stopped laughing and began to cry or should I say bawl. She was only small but did she make a din. I felt that everyone was staring at me and began to go red with embarrassment. I tried giving her a dummy but no sooner had I put in in her mouth than she took it out with such a tug it almost flew over the churchyard wall. I finally arrived home feeling tired, exhausted and humiliated.

"Where've you been?" cried Mother undoing the buttons of her blouse, "she's dying with hunger, she wants her tittie, she'll have convulsions."

"I'll have convulsions if she doesn't stop." I answered, and for a moment I wondered whether all the time I'd spend wishing and hoping for a baby had been worth it. I went outside in a huff but soon my conscience began to prick; I walked into the kitchen and there was Mother holding the baby, who was by now as peaceful as could be. I wondered how it was possible that only minutes before that same little girl had stopped shopkeepers and customers alike with her screaming. She suddenly brought back some wind, spilled some milk down the corner of her mouth, opened her eyes and beamed across the room at me. We were friends again.

CHAPTER 17

The Chicken Murderer

1914 was slowly coming to an end. The nights were getting longer and the days darker. We would spend hours amusing ourselves by playing hide and seek under the old iron lamps or singing silly songs such as:

"Like a fairy, like a fairy.
　Her big shoes were number nine.
Orange boxes without topses
　Were the feet of Clementine."

We would visit the Cosy Picture House, and sometimes in Oldham Street there would be a little side show featuring the 'the Spider Lady,' It always puzzled me how they could have this huge spider with a lady's face which would smile and wink at you. I just couldn't keep away from that show.

Then, of course, there was Charter Street Ragged School with its social room where we would play games and dance. Nothing stopped us from enjoying ourselves and making the most of our play.

Winter came and with it the baby's inevitable snuffles. Mother and Dad were showing some concern, especially since Evelyn had made so much progress over the summer months. I wasn't allowed to take her out for walks and we were told not to waken her up but to allow her to wake up herself. I would sit for ages just looking at her lying there wondering if one day she wouldn't wake up. I couldn't understand why several of my friends had six or seven children in the family, yet I only had one sister and there was no guarantee that she would live very long. Evelyn wasn't the only one under the weather though. The damp nights were causing problems for my Dad's legs. Mother was constantly on at him to rest them, so when Billy began having problems with selling his lavender in bad weather, Dad suggested he help around the house; breaking lumps of coal in the cellar, putting firewood in the coal hole, sweeping and swilling the yard every day and cleaning the windows; all Dad's normal jobs. This gave Dad's legs a rest and made sure that Billy had a roof over his head and food in his stomach.

The 'MANCHESTER PALS', officially the 'Manchester Regiment', which was raised from Central Manchester. Here the new recruits are training in Heaton Park at the start of World War I.

Christmas brought its usual variety of presents and the inevitable trip to Great Grandad's where I got my usual Jaffa. The weather was cold and icy and the steep hill outside our house was giving all sorts of trouble to the horse and cart teams. One unfortunate horse had to stop after slipping on the cobbles and crashing into the railings. Soon though the frost cleared and we began to see brighter weather. My best friend at this time was Katie who lived at the "Exile of Erin". We went everywhere together and one day when I was asked to take home one of our classmates, who had been ill, Katie decided to come too. We left the little girl at her house and we were just walking down Fern Street to come home when we heard the sound of chickens and hens screeching. We had to investigate and discovered the sound was coming from behind a big, black wooden double gate. The light from the gas lamp was shining underneath.

Slowly we opened the gate, just wide enough for both of us to see what was happening. The noise was awful and what we saw was, to us, like something out of a horror film.

There on a platform was a man in a cloak with a knife gripped between his teeth. Like lightening he would grab a hen by its neck, throw the body under his armpit and holding the head firmly would slit the hen's throat. We saw three birds dealt with in this way and were speechless until we were spotted. The man ordered someone to chase us out but it wasn't needed, you couldn't see our clog irons for feathers. We ran panting all the way home.

"Mam, Mam, we've just seen an old man murdering a lot of hens," I cried.

"Calm down," she answered, "now what's this about, someone murdering hens?"

I described what we had seen.

"Well", said Mother, "that old man was a Rabbi and he was killing the hens for the Jewish Sabbath. The Jews only eat hens that are blessed by the Rabbi and that's one of the ways he blesses them, it's called Kosher."

I couldn't understand why they didn't simply use Holy Water like our church did.

Baby Evelyn continued to make good progress and by ten months old was walking. Mother started to feed her on pobs; bread dipped in milk. She loved a crust from the corner of the loaf, dipped in milk and then in sugar, but often than not the pobs would give her an attack of wind. Mother would dash for a cup of water and sugar, grab the tongs from the fireplace, take a red hot cinder out of the fire and drop it into the cup. When the ash had settled to the bottom and the cinder had stopped sizzling, she would remove it and give Evelyn the warm sugared water. This was cinder tea and within seconds the wind would be cleared. How the baby loved it.

I couldn't understand why Mother went to all this trouble when Evelyn still seemed contented to feed on breast milk. Little did I know that Mother was doing it because she was pregnant again.

The war was still raging and we were becoming more aware of what was happening abroad. We had become used to the blackout and large posters of Lord Kitchener with his pointed finger and the phrase 'Your King and Country need you', were appearing all over the place. Thousands of men had already gone abroad but it seemed we needed a lot more. The Derby scheme was started and men were gathered together as the Manchester Pals.

One evening the air was filled with the sound of breaking glass; we all became very nervous as groups of men toured the area breaking windows in property belonging to foreigners. Rossler's had bricks thrown at its two large windows and a Jewish family on Rochdale Road received similar treatment. This was a terrible shame since the families had long since settled in England and had made Manchester their home. The Jewish family even responded with a placard in the broken window saying 'Please, I am a British subject.' Only one person seemed to benefit from this retribution and he was the man who mended the windows.

Mick, Billy, Jimmy and Johnny were all eligible for recruiting and became more preoccupied with the war. Johnny, who still managed a broad smile and a cheery good morning, was the first to receive his call-up-papers. He was required to report for service after the customary medical.

"I'll join the Pals," he said "the Manchester Pals."

He looked so smart and handsome as he threw his kit bag over his shoulder and said his goodbyes.

"Cheerio Mary," he said ruffling my hair.

"We'll be here when you come back," Dad answered.

I began to realise more and more that the war wasn't only in other countries, it was there in our house. I prayed for Johnny each night, but to no avail.

With thousands of others he was sent to the Somme and was slaughtered before he completed three months service. So, despite the song, our Johnny didn't come marching home.

Evelyn became my constant companion. I would join my friends skipping holding one end of the rope with one hand and the pram with the other. "You don't have to bring that baby all the time, do you?" they would ask. But whenever possible, wherever I went Evelyn went too.

One warm sunny June day I was playing with my sister when Mother joined us, her arms laden with nighties, napkins, skips and head shawls.

"Who are you giving those to?" I asked.

"No-one," replied Mother, "They are for the new baby."

I gasped, looking first at Mother and then at Evelyn. So we were to have another baby. What if this one cries like Evelyn, I thought, and what will my pals say. They won't play with me if I have two crying babies. I decided to pray to St. Anthony again in the hope that could convince God to make a better job of this one.

CHAPTER 18

Another Sister

June 3rd, 1915, was the King's birthday; but the date took on even greater significance in our house when my second little sister was born. You could tell straight away that she had come from Heaven; but for the absence of wings I could have sworn she was an Angel. She stretched, yawned and slept a lot and I immediately fell in love with her. We called the baby Ellen.

It seemed my prayers had been answered when she turned out to be much quieter than Evelyn. She had to have real tummy ache or wind spasms before she cried, and even then cinder tea would be the only remedy needed. At six months old though, Baby Ellen did have difficulty cutting her first tooth. She had bouts of hotness and feverishness which even sugared water couldn't cure; so Mother sent me along to the chemist for syrup of squills, syrup of violet, oil of almonds and some ipecacuanha which we called ecky pecky wine. The resulting violet coloured potion was very sweet and, with that and wintergreen oil rub, the pain eased.

In very much the same way Mother cured Ellen and Evelyn's colds using goosegrease. Katie's mother had cooked a goose for Christmas and she had given us all the leftover grease which we had put in a large jar. This was warmed on the top of the fireplace and massaged into the babies' backs. They would scream the place down but the treatment was continued until the children smelled like two fried chickens, and their colds were cured.

I was dividing my time between the children and school and there was no question about which of the two gave me most pleasure. I hated school but in spite of that I was a pretty bright child and won a Prayer book prize for an essay on 'How I spent my summer holidays'. I never received the prize though. The Irish priest wouldn't give it to me because I didn't attend church on Sunday mornings.

"The book will go to someone who will make better use of it." He declared.

Both Father Murphy and Sister Theresa showed a marked dislike for any of their school children who hadn't been compelled by their parents to attend church. And they had never forgiven us for fraternising with the 'other side' - the protestants from the local Sharp Street Ragged School. There we were made most welcome and treated to bread and treacle in the big social room with a piano. We had a marvellous time - until we were reported.

The following day we were in one of the four classes working separately in one large schoolroom when suddenly Father Murphy burst in. After a conversation with Sister Theresa he turned towards us demanding that all those who hadn't attended Mass on Sunday stand up.

Slowly and gingerly a group of us made our way to the front of the room.

"Now," Father Murphy began. "will ye all take a look at these heathens. They can't go to their own church but they can sell their souls for a round of bread and treacle."

He asked us all individually whether both our parents were Catholics and after what seemed like an age we were allowed to sit down. When I told my Mother that night she was absolutely furious and it took my Dad all his time to prevent her from going to the school to see him. I never forgot this incident and neither did my Mother. Some three weeks later I was given a long narrow piece of cardboard with 12 little envelopes on it. This was called St. Joseph's Penny and we were supposed to ask people to put at least a penny into each envelope so that the school could collect money to send missionaries to Africa. I asked my Mother if she had any money she didn't want.

"What's it for?" she demanded.

"Its to send the missionaries to Africa so that they can make the heathens into Christians."

Mother's face went red then purple.

"Heathens in Africa..... Heathens in Africa. Get me a pen and some writing paper."

She sat down and began to write.

"Father Murphy, if you have any money over after you've been to Africa to make heathens into Christians don't forget I've got three heathens here."

She folded up the St. Joseph's Penny Card, put it in an envelope and said.

"Give Sister Theresa that!"

I'm sure that from then on I became a marked pupil. I certainly thought so years later when I took part in the school concert at the Derby Hall. It was a production of 'Old King Cole' and I was a cook. The show ran for five nights and as a treat for the young performers we were promised, at the end of the run, a trip to the opening of a

Young boys assembled outside Wood Street Mission prior to a seaside trip. Organised trips were often a child's only chance of a day out, and a treat that had to be earned.

new picture house in Manchester - "The Piccadilly". and even better. we were due to go in the afternoon and miss school.

After lunch those of us from the concert party lined up to collect on our way out a bag of sweets from Sister Theresa. When my turn came she stopped and stared.

"Where were you this morning?" she demanded.

"My Mother was ill Sister...." I began.

"Well how is it she's not ill now?"

Before I had time to answer she ordered me back to my desk and instructed me to do all the sums I'd missed on the morning. I couldn't believe my ears but somehow I managed to hold back the tears as I joined the rest of the class still wearing my blue frock and white socks and shoes.

When I got home Mother was a little better and asked if I'd enjoyed the pictures.

I tried to hide my face but burst out crying, the tears falling down my dress. I blurted out the whole story.

My father couldn't conceal his anger.

"That woman must be a throw back from the inquisition," he raged.

Billy was the next to receive his call up papers. We couldn't believe it, Billy had never poked a fire, never mind used a gun, but he showed no surprise when he read the letter; he was almost resigned to joining up.

"Now that I'm going, why should England tremble," were his words to us, as he shook hands and said goodbye.

The next one to go was Jimmy, his papers arrived on Evelyn's birthday. Mother was the first to seem the as she sorted through Evelyn's cards "Jimmy" Mother shouted holding out the envelope, "I say Jimmy."

He knew instinctively what she was holding even before he opened it. "Ne'er mind. I'll get a shilling a day for this," he said walking back to continue his wash.

So now Johnny, Billy and Jimmy had all left Angel Meadow and things didn't quite seem the same. I would have missed them even more if it hadn't been for the two babies.

Evelyn was suffering with a wheezy cough and even goosegrease couldn't ease it. Mother and Dad were awake all night and eventually the doctor was called and he diagnosed whooping cough. It confirmed my Mother's worst fears. She was satisfied that Ellen, being a strong baby would get over it; but she was worried about Evelyn catching it in case her weak heart couldn't stand the strain.

The orders were to keep the two apart and to keep Ellen away from smoke and give her as much fresh air as possible. Trying to keep the babies apart was impossible so we just had to hope that Evelyn wouldn't become infected.

The weather was getting better and I was allowed to take the children out in their pram. Mother had seen a pitch cart in Ashley Lane doing the sets so I went out in search of it. I would stand in the right position, depending on the direction of the wind, and wait for the man to take a big ladel full of hot pitch and pour it onto the ground. The fumes would blow straight in our direction and we would all inhale. It must have been a good remedy for the childrens' coughs and colds, sometimes there were so many mothers with their babies in prams you had to jostle to get best force of the pitch fumes.

Despite that remedy, at the end of April Evelyn started whooping. We crossed our fingers and hoped, and by May both of them were cured and looking forward to the warmer weather, and so I was especially since it was also time once again for the processions.

CHAPTER 19

The Whit Walks

One of my favourite times each year was Whit Week. Living so close to the centre of town I could go and enjoy the colourful processions making their way round the streets to the music of brass bands.

The first to hold their Whit Walks were the Protestants. They always chose Monday and on that particular day in 1916 the weather was lovely. I decided to take the two girls, Evelyn walking at my side and Ellen in a push chair, and we made our way to the corner of Market Street and Corporation Street where someone had assembled rows of forms. We could hear the bands approaching long before they turned the corner of Deansgate and as soon as the first band came into sight everyone started to clap.

All the local schools were represented, with the children dressed in their Sunday best. There were gorgeous little girls wearing pretty summer dresses and carrying long handled straw baskets filled with fresh flowers, and little boys dressed as sailors saluting to the cheering crowd. I always used to feel sorry for the mothers who had painstakingly whitened their children's shoes only to find that the heat had melted the pitch on the road, and by the end of the day their feet were covered.

After the children came the men carrying the large tapestry banners in between two heavy brass and mahogany poles. These marvellous displays of colour bewitched everyone.

I was particularly waiting to see some of my friends who went to St. Oswald's and St. James's on Rochdale Road and my friend Lily who would be walking with Collyhurst Weslyans.

I asked the lady next to me, who had a programme,and she told me they would be along anytime. The St. Oswalds banner was just coming into sight when a voice from below cried.

"I want to pee."

It was Evelyn.

All around me people were shouting

"There's our Tommy...... Tommy... yoo hoo Tommy"

"That's mine there in the purple frock"

Evelyn was totally disinterested and continued to rock from one cheek to another.

Then I spotted Lily.

"Look, there's Lily" I said.

"Wave to Lily"

"I don't want to" she answered.

"I want to pee"

I continued to shout trying to attract Lily's attention; whilst Evelyn was busy trying to attract mine. Slowly the school passed by and I turned my attention to Evelyn who by now was going red in the face. I turned to make a way through the crowd but to my amazement found that I was fastened in by people at least three deep. I had to make a quick decision so there and then I moved the push chair to try and hide Evelyn from view, dropped her drawers and she at last relieved herself. I was all over before the next school arrived and I'm sure no-one was any the wiser.

After what seemed like an age the end of the procession was in sight. We'd seen brass bands and children, soldiers and banner bearers and slowly one by one the crowd began to disperse.

"I'd like to see cat'lics beat this on Friday" I heard one man say.

"The'll be hoppin' mad that t'weathers been nice" was the reply.

"Still they've all week to pray."

We made our way back to Angel Meadow feeling absolutely exhausted.

The Roman Catholics had their procession the following Friday and once again I set off early to make sure that I could get as good a seat as I had had on the Monday. This time though I was by myself. Mother had said that I couldn't take the babies because I'd kept them out too late, so instead Grandad gave me a silver threepenny bit to spend on some ice-cream.

I had arrived at about 7.30.a.m. and by an hour later I'd been joined by two friends of mine, Tessie and Kittie. We sat waiting patiently for the first band to appear. We knew that they couldn't be far off when the mounted policeman came by ensuring that people were in their right places. The crowd began to anticipate the beginning of the procession.

"I do hope our Damien's shoes are alright" I heard a woman say.

"Only they were pinching him a bit this morning"

She couldn't have done much about it anyway because by then the first school had appeared. It seemed to me that someone had been praying hard because the weather was beautiful.

Three Irish priests led the first school, wearing tall hats, carrying long canes and each with a gold watch chain across their ample middles. The children followed next but unlike the protestants there were no crinolines or little boys in sailor suits; the girls wore long white dresses with a blue ribbon carrying the medal of the Virgin Mary round their necks, and the boys wore white shirts with red and white sashes round their waists.

There was no shouting from the crowd and no waving to mum and dad at the side of the road, everything was just right even down to the singing of the 'The Minstrel Boy' or some other Irish tune.

The only exceptions to the rule were the Poles, Ukranians and Italians. They were allowed to wear their national costume and they gave the parade a splash of colour. The children wore embroidered blouses and skirts and had a ring of flowers on their heads, and coloured shoes on their feet and the men wore embroidered waistcoats and carried on their shoulders the very beautiful but exceedingly heavy madonna.

The figure was fixed on a solid wood plinth with four protruding poles at each corner. The men would take it in turn to carry the statue which was decked with fresh lilies picked that same morning. Then came two Italian women with their fantastically embroidered head shawls with fringes round the edges and lovely lace aprons over their black skirts. This was the end of the procession and it was always the part we enjoyed the most. As we began to make our way home we could hear a loud voice saying.

"You would think we were in bloody Ireland, wouldn't you. Why the 'ell don't they play something English".

So that was White week. Protestants on Monday with all the latest war songs and children dressed in anything colourful, and the Catholics on Friday well ordered, in their white shirts and dresses, putting down their feet with great intent and purpose to the tune of 'Father O'Flynn'.

The exceptionally hot Whit was an indication of what was to follow in summer. The nights were short and the days were long and we would spend every possible moment enjoying the fresh air. Mary Anne wasn't so lucky, The longer days meant longer hours at work and the strain was telling on her. She was loosing that straight back look which I had always admired her for and she no longer had the strength to rub her tobacco anymore. She even had difficulty holding her pipe in her hands which were now lumpy at the joints and her 'housemaids knee' was developing into a severe attack of rheumatism, it seemed wrong that she should be crippling herself for two and six a day.

Ada and Henry were still living with us and I would occasionally take Ada to the pictures. I loved Tom Mix in thrillers like 'The Hidden Hand' but Ada was more interested in the war newsreels, with their stories of the boys in Gallipoli and the Dardinelles. She was worried about her son Michael and was overjoyed when one day he unexpectedly arrived home on leave.

Their joy soon turned to sadness though when Michael told them that he had fallen in love and was planning to marry. This in itself wasn't the reason for Ada and Henry's sadness though, he told the girl that he had no parents and was now worried that if he revealed the truth her parents would stop the marriage. He hadn't been able to confide in anyone and now sought my fathers help. Father told him to go ahead with the wedding and explained the predicament to Ada and Henry. They accepted that their way of living whilst acceptable to the residents of the lodging house might not be so to Michael's future wife.

The wedding went ahead in Blackpool where the girl's parents lived, and on his demob the couple went to live in Stockport. Michael notified his mother and father of their address but Ada and Henry promised not to visit them at least until they had settled down. Michael and his new bride were never far from Ada and Henry's thoughts, even though their other son Joseph married a local girl who became one of the family. They were constantly seeking advice from dad who on one occasion casually suggested that things might be better if they moved out of the lodging house into a nice furnished room.

Ada and Henry took it to mean that they were being asked to leave, and seemed rather choked at the suggestion.

"I'm not asking you to leave" said Dad

"I'm making a straightforward sensible suggestion, you'll probably be here longer than us."

At this I felt a funny sensation in my stomach. My father must have noticed something was wrong and asked me what the matter was.

"Dad ... Are we leaving.... Are we leaving Angel Meadow?"

He nodded.

"But I don't want to leave" I protested.

"I want to stay here with Mary Anne and Little Ada, with Ada and Henry, Lizzie and Tom and Mickie and Priscilla and Bill."

It was to no avail. Father had decided that we were leaving and within three weeks we had packed our bags once again.

CHAPTER 20

On the move again

It wasn't long before we were ready to move.

All of us, except Dad, were sad to be leaving the lodging house even though we were only moving to Red Bank, about quarter of an hour away up the hill.

Slowly we began transferring things from Angel Meadow. On the first night it was some tools, a brush and a shovel and straightaway I began to clean up. As time went on the house in Red Bank was fitted out with furniture carefully transferred from Angel Meadow. It was a lengthy procedure since Dad had to be extra careful not to hurt his legs. The slightest knock would cause them to bleed and he would be rushed to hospital.

On the day before we were due to leave I got three great surprises. The first of them came from Mary Anne. Because of her worsening rheumatism and arthritis she had been working less and less. Almost apologetically she approached Mum and Dad.

"I've got a little room in Red Bank near to you" she said.

"I hope you don't mind I wanted to be near you."

I was overjoyed; and there was more to come. Ada and Henry revealed that they had finally taken Father's advise and bought a furnished room and co-incidentally, or maybe otherwise, it turned out to be in the next block to ours in Red Bank.

We were hardly surprised when Esther and Ernie also told us they too had found a place and it was only a stones throw from our new house just down the hill near the Jewish Bakers.

It was almost Christmas when we all finally moved into our new homes in and around Red Bank. Mary Anne was working again and had given my Mother the key for her little house so that I could light her fire for her. I built up a lovely roaring fire and walked home. Mary Anne had called into our house on her way home from work and was enjoying a cup of tea and a sandwich. You could tell she was already missing the company but, wanting to show her independence said she had only called in to see if we'd straightened up.

After that she visited us less and less, but I made frequent visits to see her and each time she would tell me she was "managing all right."

The Whit Walk (see Chapter 19). Courtesy of Mrs Dunne, Manchester Polytechnic.

Her attic flat was the cheapest in the house and, as there was no gas laid on, it was lit by an ordinary gold flame oil lamp. It was a far cry from her fourpence a night room at Angel Meadow with its clean beds, hot and cold water, light and heat but to Mary Anne and Henry and Ada downstairs it was home.

Christmas day came around again and with it the customary joint of pork from Rosslers the butchers. Mother served out an extra portion for Mary Anne, and after covering it with a spare plate and wrapping it in a towel, asked me to take it round to her flat,

"Don't tell Ada and Henry" she called.

"I can't afford dinners for everyone."

I went down the street to 133 and up the stairs to Mary Anne's.

"Mary Anne.... Mary Anne, its Mary" I cried.

"Open the door."

For a moment there was complete silence then the handle turned part way and sprung back.

This went on several times without a sound from Mary Anne.

I began to get worried.

"What's the matter Mary Anne, open the door."

"Just a minute I'll have another try, I can't quite manage it with my Rheumatics"

The door opened to reveal an almost completely dark room. The only light came from a faint glow in the heart of the fire, which was having very little effect against the cold winter weather. I put fresh coke on the fire as Mary Anne tucked into her Christmas lunch.

"Your mother shouldn't have bothered" she apologised.

"I was sorting something out for myself when I got round to it."

I asked her about the fire.

"Oh, I've plenty of coke" she replied.

"But I've lost my grip and I can't pick up the shovel.

The fire had begun to pick up and was bringing a little warmth to the place as I left to go home for my own dinner. May Anne gazed at me through her dull and lifeless eyes and smiled.

Around this time I began suffering from headaches and dizzy spells and, as I was only thirteen my mother and father began to worry about my health and took me to the doctors. He said it was 'my age' and I would be all right when I 'started.' I couldn't understand what I was supposed to be 'starting' but I continued to take Indian Brandy and Penny Royal in the hope that something would happen. It didn't and I worsened. I became as thin as a sheet of paper and I developed acute tonsillitis.

My father took me along to the Clinical Hospital known as the Old Northern, down Cheetham Hill Road, near Bridge Street. I was taken in to see a Doctor Mumford who asked me to climb onto a trolly. A nurse at either side gently held my hands as the doctor opened my mouth and put an ether soaked piece of lint on a piece of wire into it. I began to kick, knocking the wire from the doctor's hand, but the nurses eventually restrained me by gripping my arms tightly and sitting on my feet, in seconds I was in oblivion.

How long I remained in that state I don't know but when I finally came round I was lying on a large rubber mat with other children at either side of me and I could feel blood running down the side of my cheek.

No sooner had I opened my eyes than I was dressed and allowed out of hospital. My Father and I began the short walk home but I was still coughing blood so he had to carry me.

The following day my throat was still as sore and I couldn't swallow but as the days went on I was taken back into the hospital where Doctor Mumford suggest that I might be starting with a tubercular throat. He recommended me to another little hospital in Garden Lane, Greengate, Salford. It was called Greengate Dispensary and as if to make up for my short visit to the Old Northern Hospital the dispensary became my home for the next twelve months.

CHAPTER 21

My First Job

Apart from Sundays when I was allowed to go home to see my Mother and Father and two sisters I spent the whole of the next twelve months at the Greengate Dispensary in Salford making many new frieds.

My throat finally cleared and although I was still waiting to 'start' and suffering from headaches I was told I could go home for good. The war was four years old and I was eagerly awaiting my birthday when I could leave school and begin work.

I had a job lined up at a furniture makers called Goughs where my father knew a french polisher, and I began helping him to polish the furniture before it was sold. I would prepare a thick brown mixture in a large iron pan and dip in pieces of white wood. They would be completely submerged and then carefully taken out, having been transformed into a cholocate shade of brown. When each piece had dried I would lightly sandpaper it and using a cotton wool pad dipped in varnish polish it with several strokes of the pad. The process would be repeated and then a final coat of varnish applied. I enjoyed the work but the fumes from the methylated spirits and shellac we used gave me headaches again and I was sadly forced to leave.

I went from there to a rubber factory in Hulme where my father was working and started as a ball-inflator making rubber balls. It was a novelty for me to go to work with my Dad and I was very happy in my work, but again fate intervened and, after another accident with his legs Dad was rushed to hospital and had to hand in his notice. As I wasn't allowed to travel such a long distance by myself I had to finish.

My friend Florrie and her mother were working at a hat and cap factory near Strangeways jail and I decided to join them there. I'd never used a sewing machine before but as they needed a cap quilter machinist I picked it up very quickly. As a new girl I became the focus of attention and was always having my leg pulled, and fell for everything, including asking the mechanics for such things as a glass hammer, a few rubber nails, some double headed screws and a left handed screw driver. I even asked to borrow a Fool set and when told that the girl who had come down for a long stay had taken it I believed every word.

Soon though I began to become used to their jokes and laughed along with them. I was on piecework, the pay being one shilling a gross for the common work and one and eleven pence for the best and although we worked hard for every single penny we enjoyed it.

I was becoming more conscious of my appearance and I spent my spare money on things like threepenny tins of Eastern Foam Cream, or a twopenny tin of Phulnana Face Powder or maybe a small bottle of Ashes of Roses. After a good scrub with carbolic soap at Red Bank Baths I felt as glamorous as Theda Barra.

The highlight of the week for us was Friday, which we called Amami night after a new lovely hair shampoo; each Friday night after washing my camisoles and bloomers,and doing the housework I shampooed my hair and, when it was dry, tied it in a bun fastened with a Woolworth tortoiseshell comb - didn't I look just like Clara Bow. Everything was tuned to finish just before nine so that, at that time, I could have a natter with Mabel,who lived next door.

We would each go to the adjacent outside lavatories at the pre-arranged time and provided no-one had got there first, seat ourselves on the toilet and begin our conversation. As there was a large gap in the wall dividing the two toilets and we had little difficulty communicating and our conversation covered anything and everything, but we always included an assesment of the latest film stars wooing the audiences at the Shakespeare Picture House up Cheetham Hill Road.

On one occasion Mable mentioned Owen Moore.

"Oh yes" I replied.

"He could put his shoes under my bed anytime"

I heard a cough and my fathers voice,

"Who are you talking to Mary, you sound as if you're in confession".

I slowly lifted up the latch, and as I walked out dad walked in. I was praying he hadn't heard what I'd said.

"I was talking to Mabel" I whispered.

"Well it wasn't Mabel putting her shoes under someone's bed" he replied with a smile on his face.

"And whoever the fella is I'm sure he must be very honoured knowing he is being discussed in such distinguished surroundings."

Father needn't have worried I was still very naive about the facts of life, and so were most of my workmates. When Mabel and I walked down Cheetham Hill Road we had to walk past the old warehouse on New Bridge Street which had been converted into a hospital for treatment of venereal disease.

We never mentioned anything about it to our parents so the only pic-

Bustling Market Street in about 1920. Note Lyons Cafe on the right.

ture we got was one painted by some of our friends, and elder brothers and sisters. What they told us sounded horrible so each time we approached the hospital we crossed over the other side of the road so as not to pick up the disease.

One day Gladys, one of the girls at work came in with a "secret book". As we all tried to find out what it contained there were outbreaks of giggles all round the room. When we stopped for dinner we gathered round in a tight circle and Gladys produced the book. It was called "Aristotle's Works" and it contained explicit pictures of the development of a foetus; in turn, we read out passages. This went on until our boss Abe interrupted us. We felt so ashamed and from then on kept even further away from the VD clinic and became very dubious about the male sex.

In November the war finally ended and everything was heaven. The world became a different place with church bells ringing out and everyone dancing the Tiger Rag in the streets. The men who had packed their bags and dressed in Khaki were now returning in their demob suits, with smiles on their faces, after four years of bloody conflict.

For most of them the war was now over but for some, those who suffered terrible injuries fighting for their country, the war, like their pain, lingered on. In the hospitals and homes for the war wounded many were not allowed to forget.

Mary Anne had been fighting her own war; against crippling rheumatism which had now spread to her legs.

Her once rosy cheeks were now permanently pale and her hair, which she had always kept neatly tied in a bun was now hanging limply behind her ears. She looked cold and underfed and matters would have been much worse if not for the allocation of coal she received from the 'parish', the equivalent of todays social security. Her cat had been put down because she had no money to feed him and from her appearance it looked as if she could hardly feed herself. She was barely capable of doing the simplest of household jobs and was finding utmost difficulty in keeping herself warm. Even this presented problems as she burnt holes in a succession of items she had tried to use as blowers. The tin tray had a neat hole in the centre and charred remains of newspapers littered the grate. The ashes hadn't been cleared for days and were preventing the fire glowing with warmth. It was a pitiful sight but still Mary Anne refused to be admitted to hospital. Even with all its disadvantages the damp, dark whitewashed room with its little black fireplace was her home and that was all she wanted. It wasn't to be though; one morning mother went to check if she was all right, the door could now be opened from the outside and she went straight in. Mary Anne was lying still on the bed her eyes fixed to the ceiling. She noticed my mother enter and managed to smile.

"I can't move" she whispered.

"I can't get out of bed."

Mother called the doctor and Mary Anne was immediately transferred to the workhouse..... her last remaining wish had been to remain in her own bed but it wasn't to be.

Mary Anne died a short time later.

CHAPTER 22

Another New Arrival

After Mary Anne's death I had more time to spend with my friends and workmates. Having read 'Aristotle' with its vivid accounts of life, and especially sex, we all thought we were women of the world. To us, life centred around Red Bank, Dyson's Dance Hall, our place of work, and all the local picture houses; the Bijou or By Joe as we called it. The Temple, The Shakespeare, The Premier, The Greenhill, The Globe and the Riviera.

With all that was going on I hardly noticed that some five years after Ellen had been born my mother's figure was once again altering.

I visualised the pictures in 'Aristotle's' book and wondered about the baby lying inside her. I tried to guess how long it would be before the baby was born but she was wearing so many skirts I couldn't tell. I looked at her rounded figure and then at mine. I was now sixteen still suffering from headaches and still waiting to 'start'. My chest was flat and no matter how much I ate I still looked like Cleopatra's needle. I envied Florrie for her golden blond hair and her cornflower blue eyes but most of all I envied the two lumps which were now appearing on her chest.

That was the least of my worries though as Mother grew fatter and Father became more troubled with his legs. One night I disturbed him when he was changing his dressing. This he always did in the parlour, when Mother was out and the house was quiet.

As I entered the room he was resting his legs on the stool in front of the fire; one of them was wrapped in a bandage and covered with his woollen drawers, the other was bare.

I cringed as I saw for the first time what was causing the pain. There were three large deep ulcers and the skin was covered in eczema.

"Dad" I cried,

"How do you manage to walk with that leg? Is the other one as bad?"

"Worse" he answered.

"It's worse Mary. The only time I'll be free of pain will be when I'm dead!!"

I felt my eyes fill up and I longed to put my arms around him, somehow I couldn't. I'd never kissed my father and he'd never kissed me I wanted

Evelyn, aged four.

Nellie, aged three.

to let him know that I cared but I couldn't think of anything to do so I did absolutely nothing.

As we approached the end of the year baby clothes began to appear and I realised that Mother's time was getting near. My father had, for weeks, been saying that he wanted a son and he had already decided on a name. It was to be James Lionel. James after himself. Not, mind you, Jimmy, it had to be James; and Lionel after a sign above a shop my father remembered from his visits with a friend in Piccadilly.

On the nineteenth of October the baby was born it was a beautiful baby boy and he was of course christened James Lionel. Mother, as usual, had had a hard time and her sister, my aunt Maggie had come to look after the children whilst Dad and I were at work. It was one of the finest events ever to happen in our family and all that Mother had been through was worth it just to see the look on my Dad's face and to hear him say

"Well, I've got everything now that I've got a son"

"He's the model of you Jimmy," people would say.

"He ought to be... I'm his father" he answered poking his thumb into his chest.

Whether it was all the excitement or all the running about I'd done I don't know but I suddenly started. I felt something strange happening and ran to my bedroom my lips were quivering and my teeth were rattling like bones; I looked in the mirror, and then at the mess and began to cry. At least, I thought, my headaches will now disappear and my chest will begin to fill out. Within a short time I had developed a bust which made even Florrie envious and my headaches had become a thing of the past.

I was certainly becoming very much a woman, not only in my physical appearance but in my mental attitude also. I was still interested in fashion and one day when a friend at work brought in some new kinds of knickers with bands across each knee fastened with pearl buttons and a back flap which you brought up to your waist, I had to have a pair.

They were made of white calico and each time I wore them I felt very important. One day I was walking down Oldham Street with Mabel when for some unknown reason I sneezed, this was followed in succession with a series of similar violent sneezes. On the final attishoo my stomach expanded and I felt the button on my bloomers shoot off. Simultaneously I put a handkerchief to my nose and my other hand clasped my dress. Mabel began to laugh as I grasped my stomach tighter and tighter. We hurried past Littlewoods and the Piccadilly Picture house and into Tib Street. As soon as we came to a reasonably quiet shop we dashed in, straight past the two male assistants who had just begun to approach us, to the female salesgirl behind the counter. Mabel whispered to her, as I maintained the grip on my skirt, much to the amazement of the two male assistants.

"Well I'll have to ask the manager" the salesgirl answered Mabel. By this time the two lads were laughing heartily and I was desperately trying to hold on to my slipping dignity.

The manager arrived and allowed me to use the toilet at the back of the shop. I adjusted myself and we left the shop without giving as much as a glance to the smiling assistants. From then on we tried to avoid Tib Street, when possible and I stayed clear of knickers with buttons.

We had seen another Christmas and New Year and I was still working at the cap works. Dad was working as night watchman at the Victoria buildings in Deansgate, known as the Victoria Arcade. He would inspect all the offices when the workers had left and report to the police and fire stations before settling down to his evening in the very small narrow office with a telephone on the wall. He was his own boss and enjoyed his job, and all the workers liked him too. At Christmas they had organised a collection for him and handed over five pounds which he had in turn spent on a couple of sacks of coal and some extra Christmas presents.

I was enjoying my new experiences, and I became more aware of the other sex; particularly one young man called Harry. He was blonde with straight hair and had a slight turn in his eye which to me was rather fascinating. He wore his bowler at a jaunty angle and carried an evening paper on his way home from work. I remembered the song, "I'm Just Wild About Harry" and I thought I really was wild about him. Harry and his pals would meet us outside the roller skating rink on Thomas Street up Cheetham Hill Road. We would call at the chip shop and then Harry would take me home, leaving me just round the corner from our house. I was always in for eleven o'clock, especially when Dad was on his day off when he would wait patiently on the doorstep for me.

Time flew by and soon the collections began again for the Christmas Clubs. Each week we paid threepence, sometimes more, for a variety of Christmas gifts. As the amount saved in the Christmas fund grew, so preparations for the festive season began. Dad, in spite of his legs, decorated the parlour and Mother, who had been saving herself, bought a new peg rug from May's pawnshop on Rochdale Road. The nights were cold and long and I spent many hours sitting by the fire with Mother who had taken to having a drink of hot beer. Like Grandad, she would put the poker in the fire until it was red hot, then take it out and plunge it into a jug of beer. I used to heat the poker for her and I remember her telling me on one occasion to cover the hole in the fire.

"What do you mean Mother?" I asked inquisitively.

"Cover the hollow in the fire, it's bad luck - a death" she hastily replied.

On its own this could have passed un-noticed, but it was only one of a series of events which left us with a sinister feeling.

The second sign came as Mabel and I delivered Dad's dinner one evening. He had gone to work as usual and as we entered his office he beckoned to Mabel to sit down on the chair by the door and to me to sit by the fire.

"No you sit down on the chair Dad, on account of your legs." I said. "I'll sit on the table."

"All right then," he replied, "but don't tell your Mam you've been sitting on the table, it's a sign of bad luck."

He laughed, but the words echoed around in my head.

"Oh don't be silly Mary," he said reassuringly, "fancy talking about bad luck at this time of the year. Will I get a chance to see your boyfriend this Christmas?"

This last remark changed the tone of the conversation and we laughed and joked, unaware of the frightening truth which was soon to emerge.

CHAPTER 23

They Say the Good Die Young

Mabel and I returned home after taking Dad's dinner to the office and, with Mother, I was making final preparations for Christmas. As we both prepared to go to bed we heard a loud crash of glass. It was almost eleven o'clock and as Dad was at work we both set off to investigate. We checked the wash house window and my bedroom window above it and were surprised to find both intact. We couldn't see any broken glass anywhere so I went round to Mabel's and to Fogel's who lived on the other side. Neither of them had any signs of broken windows so we both finally made out way to bed. It was exactly a week to Christmas Day and the thought of Dad meeting some of my boyfriends helped me to forget the incident as I curled up in bed and fell asleep.

The following day I was up early before Dad arrived home and had started work by eight o'clock. By dinner time I was ready for the meal which Mother would get ready for me. As the one o'clock whistle sounded I'd already grabbed my coat and I was flying down the stone stairs. On my way home I stopped to buy some Christmas cards and as I passed St. Chad's Church I thought to myself - "I'll go to midnight mass on Christmas eve." As I turned into Knowsley Street I noticed Little Ada and Jim standing at our corner. Jim was wearing an old navy blue melton coat with an old November poppy in the lapel, and Little Ada was wearing black shawl and a long black skirt. She looked ill and Jim was obviously worried. I approached them and they both looked down as if they were trying deliberately to avoid my gaze. Something eventually gave Jim courage to speak.

"We've some bad news for you Mary."

"What is it?" I demanded, almost hysterically.

"May the Holy Virgin give me strength," Jim cried, "I'ts your Father.... sure the Good Lord thinks he's suffered enough and- and- well... he's dead!"

My legs buckled from under me and Jim caught me before I fell, leaning me on Fogel's garden wall. They helped me indoors where Mother was weeping and the two little girls were sitting quietly. James, oblivious to what was happening was rocking away on his wooden horse. I touched my Mother's shoulder and between loud sobs she began to tell me what had happened. It seems he had died at work, Celia and Theresa had found him.

Jim put his arm around me,

"They say the good die young, Mary," he said "Remember Jesus was only thirty-three when he died."

I couldn't see the reasoning. Jesus, I thought hadn't left a wife and family and hadn't suffered excruciating pain for twenty-two years. I felt a little arm creep through mine and turned to see little Evelyn's smiling face.

I burst out crying loudly again and continued to question Jim's logic. If Dad had been taken out of his misery in this way, why had God (and not the pedal of Dad's bike) allowed it all to happen in the first place? My mind was hazy.

When I eventually returned to work they had already heard the news and everyone was most sympathetic. I told them I would be off for a few days with Mother. I went to town to buy some black mourning clothes. As we walked back solemnly to our house Mother remembered the crash of glass and the omens and we swore they had been warning of Father's death.

After the post mortem the undertakers put Father in his coffin which we, in turn, put in the parlour under the window. Being winter it was exceedingly cold and as I looked at him lying peacefully in the coffin, I felt the coldness of death. He looked as if he were fast asleep, with no trace of panic in his face. The doctor said he had looked like that as he died, naked from the waist down with his leg leaning on the red iron fire bucket trying to stem the uncontrollable flow of blood. He had obviously realised that this was much worse than before as he had gradually allowed his mind to sleep.

As I looked at his face I remembered him telling me how, when he was a child he had been taken to the orphanage, where he hated every minute. How, at seventeen, he met my mother and got married. How he bought a second hand bike to get him to work and how he stumbled and the pedal ripped a hole in his ankle which never healed; an injury which caused him unbelievable pain and led eventually to his premature death.

I gently wiped his face and combed back the front of his greying hair.

Between my Mother; myself; uncle Willie, Dad's brother; and Mother's relatives, my father was never left alone until he was buried.

It was December 23rd, the day before Christmas eve when he was carried out of the house, shoulder high, on his way to Moston cemetery.

As we followed I looked at James, who people said was my father's reincarnation, and then at my Mother. The light had disappeared from her eyes and she was twisting a button round and round with her left hand on which she proudly wore her wedding ring. I visualised their wedding day, with Mother looking beautifully radiant and father, much taller and upright, wearing his mischevious grin.

I still couldn't believe that it was anything more than a bad dream as I entered the church. It was the first time I had been in church since going with Annie from Greengate when I was thirteen.

I remembered my father's words.

"You don't need a church to talk to God - whilst you're sitting in a church someone could by lying behind your own door dying." I brushed a tear from my eyes.

For the children's sake we tried to make the most of Christmas. We had left the few decorations strung across the kitchen ceiling and the few toys I had bought for the children, together with my Mother's present were put in three of Mother's black stockings which we hung at the foot of their beds.

Evelyn, Nellie and James were filled with excitement and showed no after effects from the tragic build up to Christmas.

Soon after we were all back to our normal routines. Being the main breadwinner I had to return to the hat factory. Willie was a great help doing the chores which normally Dad would have done, and contributing to the income by paying his rent.

Mother was much more lenient than Dad had been and provided I did all my regular chores I was allowed out every night. Although I was still quite young my thoughts were those of an adult and I smiled as a steady stream of girls at work left to get married. For some it was a white wedding with bouquets of flowers and the organ playing, but for others the difficulty in buttoning the top two buttons of a coat would signal a dash for the registrar's.

The latter had to have a month's notice and during this waiting period the girl would keep her fingers crossed (wishing that she'd kept other limbs crossed too) hoping that the Penny Royal, Indian Brandy, Quinine, Epsom Salts and Gin combined with the four hot baths a week, had done the trick. They rarely did and many of the girls entered married life with ready made families.

I knew I would be a virgin in white when I got married.

CHAPTER 24

The Unwanted Visitor

Slowly things got back as near as could be to normal, and we began to re-adjust to life without Father. The children helped to make matters easier with their constant antics; James was becoming quite a fine singer and his rendition of "Yes we have no Bananas" was a source of amusement to us all. He had come to regard Uncle Willie as his father and the two went everywhere together.

Mother too, it seemed, had begun to overcome the tragic loss of her husband she had taken to going out for a drink at night in the local pub. Occasionally Grandad came to stay with us so that Mother could stay out extra late.

One evening I arrived home from work to find the children in bed and the front door ajar. Willie was out courting and Grandad had gone to spend a few days with Aunt Lizzie so the children were alone. Mabel told me she had seen Mother going out some half an hour earlier and it appeared she had gone with Joe and Cissie Beaston to the Albion Pub across the road.

I decided to wait in the front room until closing time and took up my place kneeling on the sofa looking out of the window. First out was Jim, smoking his pipe, followed by Luke, the pavement artist. Mr Kingston from Honey Street was next, he was carrying a jug of beer which he was taking home to his dutch. Joe Beaston and his wife emerged, deep in conversation with my Mother and they walked across the road towards the house. As they entered the front door Mother introduced the man.

"This is Mick" she said.

I took an instant dislike to the man and ignored the introduction. As mother went to hang up her shawl I asked her again who he was.

"He's called Mick and he's Irish," she replied "he lives at Ryan's." That was the boarding house which took in single men. I politely asked the stranger if he would like a cup of tea.

"I don't, I don't" he answered "if ye'd something stronger I might oblige ye."

This only served to increase my dislike for the man, and I was determined not to go to bed until he had left the premises.

He began to look around the room and after a while his eyes fell onto the ceiling which had been blackened, over the mantlepiece with my rather unsuccessful attempts at lighting the fire. As if to make conversation he pointed out the blackened ceiling and almost in the same breath offered to replaster and decorate it. Mother seemed rather pleased that the room would be much lighter. I could only say,

"My Dad was going to do that".

The Irishman eventually left and Mother and I went to bed.

The following day when I returned home from work for my dinner Mick had already scraped and papered the ceiling. When I came home again at six o'clock the kitchen had been completely papered. Even I had to admit that he had done quite a good job, but I was careful not to show my reaction to him. Mother was obviously pleased and as we straightened up the kitchen she told me that she was planning to ask Mick to decorate the parlour. I felt as if I had been hit between the eyes.

"The parlour doesn't need decorating," I cried, "Dad did it just before he died."

I was sure that Dad had known he was about to die and had papered the parlour in preparation for his own coffin. To me that room was my shrine; I was determined that Mick wouldn't touch it.

"Let him paper the lobby," I insisted "but don't allow him to touch the parlour."

Mother took notice of my demands and Mick decorated the lobby and staircase. Most days he would arrive for work after I'd left the house, but one morning I came downstairs to find he had already arrived. I was rather concerned as there was no further work to do, and when I came home at dinner time and found him still sitting at the table with his cap on I realised that he hadn't arrived early at all, he had been in the house all night.

From then on Mick became a permanent visitor and used our house as a base for his work. He earned quite a lot decorating the large houses in Prestwich and Heaton Park and had a habit of spending it all on drink when he was paid at the weekend. He expected Mother to join him everytime he went out and on the few occasions when she chose to stay at home he became very demanding. I resented this domination but Mother seemed to find it rather fascinating.

This acceptable financial state of affairs didn't last long though. Gradually Mick went to work less and less and as a result he had hardly any wages. We found ourselves with less money for food and our meals became more and more basic. Uncle Willie, realising that he was now subsidising Mick's stay decided to go and live somewhere else, and both Ada and Auntie

Brother James Lionel, aged three.

With Eddie in our courting days.

Maggie cut down on their visits. Mick realising the position, made what seemed to be one last attempt at getting some work, but it proved fruitless; he ended up arguing with the boss and came home and flung his trowel and mortar board uder the sink.

This unsettled state at home was beginning to have an effect on me and found myself unable to laugh and joke with the other girls at work. At one stage I thought of leaving home but I couldn't face abandoning the children, even though the forelady at work had told me I could go and live with her.

Although I abandoned the idea for the time being I realised that before long the situation at home would force me to leave.

Mick was now pawning everything he could get his hands on to bring in enough money to feed us and for his regular drinking sessions; I'd noticed that Mother whose eyes were often blackened from Mick's beatings, had stopped wearing her beautiful sovereign brooch. When I asked her about it she just mumbled something about getting behind the with rent. Eventually, her diamond and emerald ring the one which Father had been so proud to see her wearing, also went into pawn. The language was becoming unbearable, not only from Mick but from Mother too. Both of them using words which would have been in place at the jail in Angel Meadow round the corner from Red Bank.

Things were building up to a flash point which eventually came one day when Mick had gone out. A man called to ask if we knew anyone who could repair a burst pipe for him. He'd obviously heard of Mick so I said I would pass the message on when he arrived home. The following morning I casually mentioned the visit to Mick,

"What man, what man?" he shouted evidently wanting the work.

"Where does he live, what's his bloody address?"

"I don't know," I answered calmly "you'll have to ask him."

This infuriated him more and he stormed towards me.

I began to walk towards the door having made up my mind never to speak to Mick again.

When I arrived home from work later that day he was still in a rage. I'd no sooner than walked through the door when he began his stream of abuse.

"You could have asked him his bloody address," he began "you could have come and found me if you'd wanted to, I was only in the bloody Knowsley, what was to stop you coming in and telling me?"

I looked at my Mother, and didn't answer.

"Are you bloody deaf or something did you hear me?" he raged.

I couldn't stand being so humiliated in front of the children whose faces were now white as death.

"I've never yet been into a pub" I said peacefully "and I've no intention of starting. As for looking for you; My Dad went to work."

The words caused a minor explosion.

"Work, Work.... Your Dad didn't know what bloody work was. I can earn more in a day than he could earn in a week....."

I stopped him. I wasn't going to allow him to say such things about my Dad. I glanced again at the terrified look on the children's faces.

"At least the bills were paid," I screamed. "Wages or no wages; and where are Mother's sovereigns and her jewellery. We didn't know what a pawnshop was until you came here."

Mick swore and disappeared from the room.

The following day I packed my bags and left.

CHAPTER 25

On My Own Again

Having taken the decision to leave home, I began to realise that I was now on my own. Fortunately for me fate played into my hands.

I went to live with Lilly's family who had a nice little house in Charles Street, Lower Crumpsall, not far from Levensteins Dye Works. There were no direct buses so each morning we met other girls from the factory and set off early to get into work by eight o'clock. One morning we were walking past Frost's Farm and the S.M. Shirt Factory when we were stopped dead in our tracks. There, walking towards us, was my old friend Eddie, his lunch box tucked safely under his arm. We began to talk and my friends walked slowly on. I explained that I had just left home and how Mick had been making my life a misery. He was very sympathetic but, as he was late for work, we agreed to meet again the following day and I rejoined my friends. Lilly was surprised that I should know Eddie as she had been seeing him every morning for years. She even knew where he lived and showed me his little house which was on Hawkshead Road.

The following morning we met again and after exchanging greetings we both went on our way to work. That evening on my way home, I was passing his house when he emerged from the front door and made his way towards me.

"Will you go with me to Queen's Park Hip?" he asked.

I quickly said yes and we arranged to meet. From then on we met quite regularly and he became a regular visitor to Lilly's on Sunday afternoon where we were entertained by a concert made up of Lilly's sisters. After a while I was taken to meet Eddie's family, his mother, his brothers and his sister who lived with her two children in Bradburn Street just round the corner from Eddie's house. We all got on well together and his family accepted me as another sister.

Later that year we became engaged.

I was, whenever possible, paying brief visits to my Mother's; usually on a Saturday afternoon, when 'Mad' Mick was out at the bookies. Each time Eddie would stay outside as I grabbed a few moments with James and the girls.

If Mick had found out he would have gone berserk, as he was always trying to meet me coming out of work to demand some money.

I took to using another door and managed to sneak out most days whilst he was waiting at the front gate. On the one occasion Mick caught up with me I threatened to call the police and he went away with his tail between his legs.

This constant stress was beginning to tell on me and, although I was still happy staying with Lilly's family, I began to suffer with my nerves.

But this all changed when I realised I was pregnant.

I think it was Oscar Wilde who once said.

"You can't go wrong in the country."

Eddie and I proved him wrong on one of our Saturday picnics at Sudden on the way to Rochdale. As my waist began to grow I realised that we couldn't have chosen a better place for a picnic.

Of course, Eddie and I were quite worried; especially since I now had no-one apart from him and his mother to talk to. I couldn't help remembering how my Father had looked after young Lettie and how my Mother had shown so much concern for her. I decided not to tell my Mum until after Eddie and I had been married.

When we finally picked up enough courage to tell Eddie's Mum we were both quite surprised when she took it quite calmly: it seems we weren't the first in his family to find themselves in that predicament. She told us to put the banns in at St. Luke's Protestant Church. I wasn't particularly keen on having a church wedding, since it was customary for the bride's family to foot the bill and I didn't even want Mother and Mick to know, let alone be expected to pay.

Eddie and I decided we would be married in a registry office. This wasn't good enough for his mother who was all the more insistant that her son be married in a church. I decided that the time had come to tell her the reasons for my wanting a quiet, simple wedding. She reluctantly agreed and we made it to the registry office just before four o'clock. The date was set at June 12th 1926. I bought a nice sage green cotton dress, a matching edge to edge coat and a small Glengarry hat with a feather at its side. I had tan kid gloves and a handbag, tan shoes and white lisle stockings which were very fashionable. Eddie. who was always very smart didn't need to buy a new suit, he went in his tailor-made grey.

Eddie's brother always came home from the CWS Factory on Balloon Street for his dinner, so since we had arranged the wedding for one o'clock we asked him to be the best man. He could call in at the registry office on his way home, and still have time to have his dinner and be back at work for two.

Keeping our eyes open in case Mick was passing we dived into the registry office with Eddie's brother and mother. In a couple of minutes the service was over and we were married. We left as quick as we had entered and caught the bus to Heaton Park. No-one could have guessed that we were young newly-weds. I had no bouquet and Eddie wasn't wearing a carnation. There wasn't even any rice or confetti. The only thing which could have given anything away was the look in our eyes... how they sparkled.

We jumped off the bus at Heaton Park gates and, still hand in hand, began to make our way towards the tea rooms where we could have our wedding feast. For the first time as 'Mrs' I poured out my husband's tea as we tucked into ham sandwiches and currant bread.

We walked through the flower gardens with their famous rose trees and sat on the grass making daisy chains. I put one on top of Eddie's head.

"This is your halo," I said.

"What do I need a halo for?" he asked.

"Well, you deserve a halo for what you've done, marrying me the way you did in the registry office," I replied.

"Eee, flippin'eck luv, it were nearer than Gretna Green."

We both rolled with laughter.

After a sail on the boating lake we decided to make our way home calling in at the Fish and Chip shop for some supper. Those chips tasted better than anything we'd ever had before and the vinegar, when we drank it out of the paper was like wine.

When we finally arrived home Eddie's mother was still waiting for us and we all had a glass of Elderberry wine. His younger brothers shook our hands and we went to bed.

The next day we were both back at work since we couldn't afford to miss a day's wages. Each week Eddie brought home two pounds, five shillings out of which we gave his Mum two pounds. Out of my wages I had to pay work insurance, hardware club for pots and pans, sixpence brew money, one shilling bus money and a penny for the hospital fund, and what was left I put into a big pot. I was beginning to lose time each day with bouts of morning sickness. They began dead on eleven o'clock and would just be clearing at twelve. The lost hour meant the difference between us saving or just paying our way. I was getting closer to my time.

When the news of our wedding eventually reached my Mother she sent a note to work saying how pleased she was but also how disappointed she'd been at us doing it behind her back. I decided that the time had come to see my sisters again and made arrangements to meet them the following evening after work. We chose outside Strangeways Jail so that if Mick should appear we could tell him we were waiting for a warden friend. It was good to see the young girls again and we spent quite some time talking before we made our way home. I realised that although I now had a husband of my own, and would soon have a family too, I was still very much missing my Mother, the two girls and James. I had no such feelings for Mick. He had now discovered that I was married and had suggested to Mother that I should help support the children, which indirectly meant him as well.

The girls were looking underfed and the effect of living with Mick was telling on them. It was however, making them very mature in their outlook to life.

When January 1927 came round, I was bouncing rather than walking around. I'd let out my stays as far as they would go and slit my dress a little lower at the front to disguise the bulges but there was not hiding the fact that the baby would arrive and on February 27th I gave birth to a baby daughter which we called Dorothy.

So now I had gone full circle. From being myself the first child of a doting Mother and Father, I was now in a position of being the Mother to our first child. My mind went back to Buxton, to the Lodging House in Angel Meadow and to my Father who gave everything for his family and in the end was given so little in return. I hoped that things would be different for our child, Dorothy, but also wished that many of the experiences I'd shared would be hers also.

Now I'm in my eighty-seventh year and I can look back on my early life with fond affection.

My own family grew with the birth of two sons, Granville and Tony, and with Dorothy, my daughter, they have provided me with the joy of grandchildren and great-grandchildren to whom this book is dedicated.

Nellie, the little girl who didn't like to cry and quivered her lip, is now in her seventies; she still has a quiet nature and has a daughter and granddaughter and grandson of her own.

Evelyn, the little girl who was spoiled and cried to get attention, is now a wonderful person with a very good nature. She lives with her husband in Blackpool.

James Lionel, is our younger brother, and we all keep in touch with each other.

Over the years I've witnessed the demolition and destruction of many of the places which meant so much to me as a child. Angel Meadow is no more, and the Lodging House has long since gone; but back in Buxton, where I was born in 1904 the old stone cottage is still standing...

OTHER BOOKS TO LOOK OUT FOR BY
PRINTWISE PUBLICATIONS LIMITED

Illustrations relating to the history of Manchester, Salford and Surrounding District
ISBN 1 872226 00 0   £2.99

Ralston's Views of the Ancient Buildings of Manchester (1850)
ISBN 0 904848-06 X   £2.99

Pictures of Olde Liverpool. Drawings and sketches.
ISBN 1 872226 02 7   £2.50

Manchester in Early Postcards (Eric Krieger). A pictorial reminiscence.
ISBN 1 872226 04 3   £2.50

Lancashire Halls (Margaret G. Chapman) Sketches, photographs and a short history of each Hall.
ISBN 1 872226 03 5   £3.99

Cheshire 150 Years Ago (F. Graham). Unique collection of 100 prints of the whole of Cheshire in early 1800.
ISBN 1 872226 07 8   Special Price £4.95

Lancashire 150 Years Ago. Over 150 prints reflecting early 19th century Lancashire.
ISBN 1 872226 09 4   £4.95

Ports of the North West (Catherine Rothwell) A pictorial study of the region's maritime heritage
ISBN 1 872226 17 5   £3.95

Southport in Focus. Glimpses of the town's past (Catherine Rothwell)
ISBN 1 872226 15 9   £2.50

Oldham Between the Wars. A collection of photographs from the camera of Edward and Edward Holgate Fletcher. (Edward Perry and Eric Krieger)
ISBN 1 872226 12 4   £2.95

Bright and Breezy Blackpool. A pictorial journey through Blackpool's past.
ISBN 1 872226 13 2   £4.95